Stop The BOLLOCKS!

Andrew Macleod

Contents

Introduction

Like many western countries Australia has seen a decrease in the quality and honesty of public political debate. If public political debate is poor, then the very essence of democracy is challenged – free *informed* consent.

The purpose of compiling this collection of previously published works is to add to the depth of debate and discussion – to fight back against the sound bites and the banality of the news cycle.

Andrew MacLeod.

Part One: Global Future

A: Religion, Terrorism, extremism and over-reaction

Al Qaeda is a franchise - Osama's death will not change the War on Terror.

Introduction

After 21/2 years in Pakistan, I took another view on the 'War on terror'.

Sometime in the future, scholars may look at Al Qaeda in a similar way to McDonalds. The McDonald's franchise model sees no direct 'command and control' lines between the centre in the h US, and a remote McDonalds store in Islamabad. All that is needed is an agreement to follow a certain philosophy and product range (i.e. Big Macs) and then there can be a share in profit.

Likewise with Al Qaeda. There is not always a command and control line from the centre out to a terrorist. However, if the terrorist follows a certain 'belief' to kill 'infidels', then that terrorist reaps the supposed profit, in the next world 'Paradise'.

So what now that Osama is dead?

The 'War on terror' is not like war as we used to understand it. There is no single 'front line' separating troops of opposing armies. There is no clear battlefield and no easy way to assess who is winning and who is losing.

This so called war is more metaphorical than physical. It is a clash, not of cultures, but of beliefs. And whilst troops may be visible in Iraq and in Afghanistan, and whilst Osama bin Ladan is now dead, the metaphorical frontline exists not between Christianity and Islam, nor between capitalism and tribalism, but within Islam itself. The metaphorical frontline pits radical Islam against conservative Islam, and conversely also unites radicals and conservatives against 'secular' and moderate Islam.

Pakistan is a country central to this 'war' not because of its border with Afghanistan and Iran, but because of the ideological battle that goes on within its complex mix of cultures. The 'conservative' Islamists (who may be peaceful but highly sensitive to their religious and cultural values) neither agree with suicide bombers, nor with the open expression that 'secular' and moderate Muslims accept in western values.

Pakistan's sometimes confusing model of democracy has to balance the role of the military and civilian governments. At the same time it dances the fine line of a national culture seeking equilibrium between the views of radical, conservative, secular and moderate Islamic thinkers.

To understand this, let's examine a strange analogy. Let us look at the response to the massive earthquake that struck in northern Pakistan in October 2005.

The earthquake hit six weeks before a Himalayan winter was due to strike. A population the size of Melbourne - 3.5 million people – was made homeless. Six thousand schools and 600 hospitals and medical facilities were wiped out. Snow and freezing temperatures threatened most of the survivors.

As a result the Pakistan people, Pakistan Army and International Community responded to what the United Nations now calls the best run relief operation ever. This operation kept people alive through the winter and then had to prepare the people for the forthcoming monsoon season.

When preparing the contingency plans for the monsoon season I had to meet with the Provincial Relief Commissioner of the North West Frontier Province (roughly equivalent to Victoria's Emergency Services Commissioner) who had responsibility for preparing his province (the equivalent of an Australian state). I asked him his view of the contingency plan.

"Well Andrew," he began, "you need to understand something. God sent the earthquake because the people were bad. If the people are good then the monsoon season will be alright. If the people are bad then God will punish them again. Who am I to get in the way of the will of God?"

He believed therefore that planning for the monsoons was unnecessary as it was all in the hands of God. Insha'Allah.

I returned to Islamabad, Pakistan's capital, to discuss the same issue with more moderate and secular minded decision makers. Their response was that one cannot say whether the Provincial Relief Commissioner was right or wrong, as his view was based on his belief in God. The decision makers in Islamabad believe that planning for monsoons was necessary, but they would not say that the Provincial Relief Commissioner was wrong.

And here is the metaphorical front line. As a foreigner I would never be able to persuade the Provincial Relief Commissioner that he should undertake contingency planning – even though the decision makers in Islamabad thought it was needed. This was a problem for the Pakistanis to sort out.

In Australia that there are often conflicts between Steve Bracks and John Howard on issues that they may call 'ideology' – be it the role of the State in the health, education or industrial relations systems – or even disaster preparedness and response. Australian disagreements are on a much simpler scale than the Pakistani disagreements based on the belief in and role of God.

So let us return to the front line in the metaphorical War on Terror.

If the terrorists of Al Qaeda, in Iraq, Afghanistan or elsewhere, are motivated by their particular radical version of conservative Islam, who is better placed to dissuade them? Is it the United States through military means, or is it moderate and secular Islamic thinkers through dialogue, and force where necessary?

It was not my role to dissuade the Provincial Relief Commissioner of his view of the role of God in disaster preparedness. Likewise it is not for the Americans to 'win' the war on terror by killing Osama or even by dissuading the radicals of their view of the role of God. Moderate Islam must take on this dialogue, and the American must realise the limitations to their role and the counter-productivity of hypocrisy.

Andrew Macleod spent 2 ½ years in Pakistan seconded into the office of the Vice Chief of General Staff working on earthquake reconstruction.

The Crucifixions continued all afternoon. Why would people pay to be crucified?

Introduction

In 2008 I found myself working in The Philippines for the United Nations on post disaster recovery work. I stumbled upon a religious tradition for people to pay to have themselves crucified. I wrote the article below as a result.

Multimedia (ebook only)
There is a video of the crucifixions here.

The Crucifixions continued all afternoon. Real nails hammered through real flesh into real wooden crosses. But this is not Ancient Rome, this is modern Philippines.

Much like 2000 years ago the Crucifixions did not take place on a lonely hill top, rather a crowd gathered in a carnival like atmosphere, with street vendors, helium balloons, ice cream, and a mass media gaggle. Unlike Ancient Rome though, these Crucifixions did not end in death, although pain was clearly evident.

Each Good Friday the town of San Fernando, an hour and a half drive north of the capital Manila, hosts the Maleldo festival in which the last day of Christ is re-enacted. Volunteers drag heavy wooden crosses to a hill on the outskirts of town, where they consent to being nailed to a wooded cross and raised in front of a crowd, hoping for absolution of their sins. Nails are driven through the palm, as Christ is often depicted, even though Romans drove the nails through wrists, as only the wrists are strong enough to hold people for long periods of time.

In a nod to modernity, volunteers have the hands washed in alcohol and nails sterilised before they are driven into their hands by a man dressed as a roman soldier.

Those seeking redemption hang in front of the gleeful crowd for half a dozen minutes, before the cross is lowered, nails removed, and the next volunteers await the hammer. Medical attention is given to those victims recently removed.

Others flagellate and beat themselves with whips made up of 25 wooden fingers, swinging back and forth around their bodies, click-clacking in a rhythmic beat as the wood eats away, skin shredded leaving blood and muscle on display.

Much like the Ashura celebrated in the Islamic world, mass flagellation and self-inflicted bloodshed are seen as a self-sacrifice that is believed to absolve sin.

Sin however is not unknown in this region of The Philippines. A little over 15km up the road, the town of Angeles exists on the back of the sex trade established outside the gates of the former US military base at Clarke Field. The Lonely Planet says Angeles is the home of child sex tourism. Whilst most stores and businesses are closed on Good Friday, Angeles' sex trade was up and running as normal – mainly serving western tourists.

One cannot fail to see the irony of the juxtaposition of modern day absolution of sins, down the road from modern day Sodom and Gomorrah – just one of many contradictions in this the world's largest catholic country.

However, whilst as a secular person I may well admire the devotion to faith, I do question the good sense of both the flagellation and the voluntary submission to being nailed to a cross.

Perhaps religion has served its good purposes in giving people a moral code to strive at. Yet when one considers Jesus Christ is a teacher and a prophet recognised as the most, or at least the second most, important prophet or teacher in Islam, Judaism and Christianity – yet the three religions fight over their small differences, rather than looking at the many similarities.

After all, the Ten Commandments direct each of the three main monotheist religions in which believers are told 'Thou shall not kill'. But kill each other they do.

So whilst the crucifixions will continue, as will the sex trade and suicide murderers misnamed suicide bombers, ironies and contradictions abound as we hope that as the world progresses, so will religion.

Should we question the recognition of the Catholic Church as a religion?

In October 2012 Ron Harding, the president of a bikie club targeted by a special police taskforce, made a provocative rebuttal to the government's plans to criminalise motorcycle clubs. Harding asked whether the Catholic Church should also be deemed a "criminal organisation" due to child abuse by priests. (Read more: here)

Over the years there have been many questions raised about the Church of Scientology and if it should be recognised as a religion. Many people think not.

With the current turmoil being faced by the Catholic Church around sexual abuse of children and other crimes, is it too much to ask if the institution of the church has step so far away from a moral framework that it loses its right to be called a religion? The Church would argue not.

Under Australian law, what is a religion? Does the Church comply with the definition?

Section 116 of the Constitution of Australia prevents the national government from making laws for establishing any religion, imposing any religious observance, or prohibiting the free exercise of any religion. This section has been subject to judicial review in the High Court.

In determining what makes a religion our national judges have used a number of tests. The leading case on this question remains the 1983 judgment of the High Court in Church of the New Faith v Commissioner for Pay-Roll Tax. Understandably, and perhaps cynically, religious status is a highly valuable commodity for tax breaks.

The court found that Scientology was a religion, despite some judges commenting on some of scientology's practices. In reaching this finding, the court argued that the definition of religion needed to be flexible. But the court also noted that one needs to be sceptical of disingenuous claims of religious practice.

Justices Ronald Wilson and William Deane gave five "indicia" of a religion: a belief in the supernatural; a belief in ideas relating to "man's nature and place in the universe"; the adherence to particular standards, codes of conduct or practices by those who hold the ideas; the existence of an identifiable group of believers, even if not a formal organisation; and the opinion of the believers that what they believe in constitutes a religion.

Let's unpack part of the question as it applies to the institution of the Catholic Church. I stress here that we should question the institution, not individual believers. Indeed, a betrayal of the philosophy underlying Catholicism by the institution of the Church, betrays those very believers.

How does the Church stand up to "the adherence to particular standards, codes of conduct or practices by those who hold the ideas" test? In asking we can recognise that 'a few bad apples' does not make a bad bunch. So let's look at what the structure of the church has done, rather than individuals.

More and more victims are coming forward with experience of child abuse at the hand of Catholic priests, but also coming with these accusations are claims that the Church has hidden or moved the priests out of the reach of the law. Senior police investigator Peter Fox is just one of the many voices making this claim (see here).

While a young lawyer I worked for a firm that represented Catholic Church Insurance in defending many of these priests against the civil claims. Legal professional privilege prevents me from giving specific examples, however some of the confessions priests made to us left my stomach sick. In listening to the priests I saw no evidence that would undermine Peter Fox's claims.

While an individual priest's actions could be a bad apple, the institution's decisions to move the accused out of arm's length to the law, is an institutional decision.

Frighteningly though, child sex abuse may not be the only type of crime where the Catholic Church has hidden accused, and perhaps may not even the worst of crimes. Without discounting the great evil that is child sexual abuse, the crime of Genocide is recognised as the worst evil that humanity can perpetrate on itself.

I worked in Rwanda for the International Committee of the Red Cross in the aftermath of the Genocide. Not only was there evidence of priests actively involved in the genocide, and several convictions in international courts, there is evidence of the Catholic Church moving priests out of Rwanda and into Belgium to protect them from accusations of complicity in genocide (see more here).

I also worked for the United Nations in the Philippines. Globally it is recognised that educating woman and girls, particularly in family planning issues, is a key to breaking the cycle of poverty. Bangladesh has seen enormous improvements in poverty largely by empowering women and girls with family planning decisions.

Yet in The Philippines, the Catholic Church institutionally was and is the greatest blocking force to sensible sex education programs and contraception (see more here). This single decision is keeping many women in poverty and keeping women and girls vulnerable to many health issues sometimes leading to death.

None of this of course touches on the Church's institutional hatred of the gay community, their anachronistic status as a 'nation' through the Holly Sea's role at the United Nations, the collection of multiple billions of dollars in vast institutional wealth, while still claiming charitable status to institutionally work for the poor claiming tax deductions in those same poor (and wealthy) countries.

So let's go to the question: In testing the institution's 'adherence to particular standards', what are the standards that the Catholic Church applies to its deeds not to its words? How does the Church Institution stand up to the test of "adherence to particular standards, codes of conduct or practices by those who hold the ideas"?

Given the institutional protection of paedophiles, genocide suspects, the fight against women coming out of poverty through education, the collection of vast amounts of wealth, do we still think this is an institution that sticks to its principles and is worthy of the classification as a religion? Is it now time to question the very premise of the institution that makes up the Catholic Church?

In considering the above question lets be careful to clarify what we are not saying. We are not saying that freedom of religion should be limited. We are not saying people should not be catholic.

We are saying though that the institution that makes up the Catholic Church hierarchy has been so focussed on protecting its image that it perhaps has lost focus of its purpose, and therefore we should question if the hierarchy should receive the tax and legal breaks the church hierarchy get from being classified as a religion.

Regrettably the Church is not alone. Some of what I saw while working for the UN would make you feel sick.

With what is now known about the 'food for sex' scandals by UN peacekeepers in west Africa, the UN staff roles in child and teenage trafficking into Bosnia during the war, and the goings on in places like in the Havana café, it would not surprise me if one day the UN gained a reputation a harbourer of paedophiles.

But the United Nations is not known for its forthrightness and candour in internal investigations. It has been criticized for ignoring evidence or wrongdoing in the past – including accusations of rape and murder by "peacekeepers.

"Like the Catholic Church, most early revelations of peacekeeping abuses have only been revealed by news organizations. Such was the case in Cambodia in the early 1990s and later in Somalia, Bosnia and Ethiopia.

"I am afraid there is clear evidence that acts of gross misconduct have taken place," said Kofi Annan when Secretary-General. "This is a shameful thing for the United Nations to have to say, and I am absolutely outraged by it."

Yet no major public investigation took place.

Given my work as a junior lawyer defending catholic priests against the civil claims of paedophilia, perhaps one day the UN and the Catholic Church will be challenging each other in the reputation stakes.

Would we treat the Arabs the same way?

Introduction

I spent a holiday in Yemen for New Year's Eve 2006/2007. This visit coincided with the Islamic holy day of Eid-al-Adha and was the same time that Saddam Hussein was executed. It was a time not to be a westerner in Yemen you would think. I was surprised to find it friendly and in some ways more tolerant than the West. This led me to ask the question: Would we treat the Arabs the same way? I wrote this article in January 2007 upon my return to Islamabad.

Multimedia (ebook only)

I have a video of the trip to Yemen on the last 8 minutes of this film _here_. The earlier parts of the film are also worth watching and include a trip to Iran with a Pakistan Army General. Are Muslims really as scary as some believe?

I spent New Year's Eve and the days around it in Sana'a, the capital of Yemen, and I wonder if good natured Australians would treat Yemeni Arabs in the same way that they treated me?

Clearly I was a foreigner, camera in hand as most tourists have. I wore an Akubra hat, RM's pants and belt and Redback boots. I was, I thought, clearly and Australian – but to many of the Yemeni Arabs I looked American.

Yemen is said to be a hot bed of al-Qaeda. It is where the USS Cole was bombed, has recently come out of a civil war, and is awash with weapons. Almost every man wears the Yemeni Jambiya, a curved and brutal dagger that rests in a waste belt.

Added to this, December 30 was the Islamic religious day of Eid, roughly equivalent to the Christian Christmas in that families gather to feast, swap gifts and attend sermons at the Mosques. Compounding potential problems was the execution of Saddam Hussein on the same day.

Clearly this would not be a hospitable time for an American looking Australian, a citizen of the 'Coalition of the willing', so why go?

I have had the good fortune in my work to visit many countries and seen many things. Sana'a, Yemen's capital, is a

World Heritage protected city. Its old mud brick buildings are said to be the original sky scrapers, stretching eight to ten stories and build on thousand-year-old foundations.

It is the city said to have been founded by Noah's son following the biblical flood, and is close to the site where the Ark is said to have been launched.

So there I was in an historical and religious city, in a country said to be the hotbed of terrorism, where an al-Qaeda attack had taken place and it was the Islamic religious day on which Saddam Hussein had been executed.

How was I treated?

Yemen has without doubt been the friendliest of countries that I have had the good fortune to visit. Out of the blue people would approach me on the street, and ask where I was from. When I replied 'Australia' they would warmly shake my hand and say 'Welcome to Yemen', and really mean it.

This did not happen once or twice, it happened on dozens of occasions over three or four days. On Eid day an old man even came to me, welcomed me to Yemen and gave me an ice cream for Eid. He then left, happily walking off down the street.

Others invited me into cafes to share sweet tea.

So what would the friendly Australian do on the streets of Melbourne or Sydney?

Let's say on Christmas day a Yemeni was walking the streets, camera in hand wearing the habitual clothes of his country. In place of my Akubra, he wore the keffiyeh, the traditional cloth head covering. In place of the kangaroo skin hat band he wore a fakal, the twisted rope that sits around the head and holds the cloth in place.

In place of my RM's belt he wore the broad belt and Jambiya dagger and in place of the RM's pants he wore the long flowing white Arabic robe.

How would Melbournians treat this Arab, suspiciously photographing critical infrastructure like Flinders Street Station, St Paul's Cathedral or Federation Square?

Would Melbournians offer him an ice cream, or would the fear what he was planning for New Year's Eve. Would they invite him for a cup of tea, or report him to JWH's terrorism hotline?

And if honestly we do not think we would welcome him to our country, as I was welcomed to his, what does it say about our 'civilisation', our 'mate-ship', our 'tolerance' and our 'hospitality'?

What does it say about the shape of our 'relaxed and comfortable' or our 'alert but not afraid' country that the Government has given us?

And if we would not welcome a foreigner just because he looked different, what does it say about us and our country?

I will let you be the judge.

Civilian rule – The illusion of Pakistan Democracy.

Introduction

I spent 2 ½ years in Pakistan coordinating the earthquake relief following the massive earthquake in 2005. During this time I came to learn a lot about Pakistan. I am not convinced that a corrupt civilian government is better than a military one. I wrote the below in 2008 after leaving the country, and my views have not changed as I have seen the rule of Zadari unfold.

Multimedia (ebook only)

I have three videos from Pakistan:

- How we coordinated the earthquake relief here.
- The fun and spectacular parts of Pakistan here.
- Thoughts on leaving the country here.

Pakistan is neither a democracy, nor a military dictatorship. Regardless of what transpires after the attempted returns of Benazir Bhutto or Nawaz Sharif, or whether President General Pervez Musharraf keeps or removes his military uniform, Pakistan will remain neither a democracy nor a dictatorship.

To create a genuine democracy Pakistan faces the daunting task of developing and promoting gender and economic equality. Only then it can hope to promote anything like a democracy that Australians understand.

Five components of the Pakistani society are indicative of the current state of affairs. These are the media, the courts, the civil service, the military and the political parties.

In 1999 when Musharraf took over as President in a coup (or 'counter-coup if you accept Musharraf's account of events), the international media condemned the take-over by a military dictatorship. Whilst it is not right for the military to over-turn an elected government, the government it put in place was not a dictatorship but what one could call a 'military lead' government.

Military dictatorships are normally brutal, authoritative and pay no regard to institutions of the state, let alone media, courts and civil society. Yet since coming to power Musharraf has sponsored a comparative liberation of the media and an expansion

15

of freedom of speech when compared to his two 'democratic' predecessors.

Whilst many would say that Pakistan is far from perfect, the number of independent TV channels created in Pakistan since 1999, many critical of the government, is well into triple figures.

The expansion of an independent media is not normally an indicator of a 'dictatorship'.

Musharraf's recent well publicised run-in with the Chief Justice of the Supreme Court is also demonstrative of non-dictatorial behaviour. Musharraf did not 'sack' the Chief Justice; he referred accusations of corruption against the Chief Justice to a panel of judges for review, and suspended him during that review.

The Judicial Review dismissed the charges, re-established the Chief Justice and the Chief Justice's re-instatement was accepted by Musharraf. Musharraf did not like it, but he accepted it. Is this acceptance an action of a 'dictator'?

Like India, the Pakistani Civil Service has a culture and a structure reflective of the Colonial Civil Service the British created. It is large, slow and lethargic (an accusation thrown at most civil services).

In my experience of the relief and reconstruction following the 2005 earthquake (both of which have been incredibly successful when measured against any international standards) it has been the military structures that delivered rapid results, and the civilian structures that moved too slowly. When the military attempted to hand responsibility for food deliveries to displaced people, the civilian structures failed and the military took responsibility back.

When looking at reconstruction, few if any reconstruction activities have been done by line ministries. Those that have successfully been implemented are those supported bilateral partners, donors, and supervised by the military led Reconstruction Authority. The civil service has been slow to get going. It is picking up speed now, but it took time.

Whilst rapid delivery required military involvement following a disaster, the Civil Service's institutional lethargy ensures that there is a degree of governmental conservatism that acts as a buffer to a full government takeover by the military.

The military takes a large role in government – perhaps too large – and at times acts as a 'paternalistic elder brother' to the civilian structures.

So what would be needed to move from this 'paternalism' to democracy? Would it be possible and would it be a good idea?

Two things additional to the judiciary and the media are needed: One is a functioning party system that represents people, and the other is a belief in 'one person one vote', both of which are linked by class and culture.

In Pakistan there is not a strong egalitarian nature as in Australia. There is a strong class system where political parties appear to be the preserve of the rich and influential class. Take Benazir Bhutto's 'People's Party' as one example.

Is a party led by the Oxford and Harvard educated daughter of a former Prime Minister, whose family estates cover thousands of acres – really representative of the poor and dispossessed?

In a country where even the middle class refer to their full-time drivers, cleaners and household staff as 'servants', where feudalism and clan ties still rule, can one person one vote work? Can an upper middle class man accept that his vote is 'only' worth the same as his 'maid-servant's vote?

What of the vast majority of women whose political and economic class doesn't, like Bhutto, raise her from the slums? In a country where in many villages a female will not show herself to a non-related male, how can she attend a polling station?

Given the class divide can we say the country could eventually accept one 'man' one vote, let alone 'one person' on vote?

Although it is tempting to look towards a female Prime Minister in the Islamic world as a beacon of hope and moderation, one perhaps can also see her two previous terms as Prime Minster for another indication that shows her class and not her gender to be the key factor.

She was elected on the back of her family name, fighting for political power after the military government executed her father.

Yet both her previous terms ended with her being dismissed by a civilian President for alleged corruption. She is also appealing against a conviction in the Swiss courts for money-laundering.

This corruption is perhaps a more 'realistic' symbol of what class and democracy has brought to Pakistan's political system.

Categorising Pakistan as a military 'dictatorship' is wrong. But moving to democracy is not as simple as one man removing his uniform. A true democracy in Pakistan would take the breaking of a feudal and class system, elevating women to equal status, and the fostering of economic and educational development.

It will require the slow building of faith and trust in both the institutions of government, and the people who fill those institutions.

In this context perhaps a 'benevolent dictatorship' is better than a corrupt democracy – if one can find the benevolent dictator.

When Right Flexes Might, Human Rights Take Flight

Introduction

Recent European right wing election results show that even though a decade old, this article has relevance today. It was co-written with Greg Barns following the death of European right wing extremist Pim Fortuyn.

Multimedia (ebook only)

The below article first appeared in the Sydney Morning Herald *here* on May 27, 2002.

The far right misfits of the European political stage, the assassinated Dutch extremist politician Pim Fortuyn and France's Jean-Marie Le Pen, have claimed their first scalp. According to British media reports last week, the British Prime Minister, Tony Blair, reacted to Fortuyn's party's electoral success by talking tough on asylum seekers.

Blair apparently wants the air force to carry out bulk deportation of asylum seekers who are intercepted in the Mediterranean and to deport them back to the world's most notorious danger spots: northern Iraq and Afghanistan. He also wants to push for a more hard-line stance on refugees in Europe at next month's European Union summit in Seville. All this at a time when the EU released a report last week warning that the constant identification of asylum seekers with terrorist threats is turning Europe into a racist, xenophobic region.

This caving in to the far right must be resisted if we are to prevent the liberal democratic world from collapsing into a cesspool of hatred and resentment and an inevitable end to the great achievement of the 18th century "Enlightenment" - the universality of human rights.

The answer to the rise of intolerant rightwingism is to reinvigorate and defend the institutions and values that are under attack. Take multiculturalism, for example. In Europe, as in Australia, the trend has been to recognise that a society functions better when the individuality of communities is respected and enhanced, leading to a greater benefit to the collective and to the individual. If we are truly committed to the core values of tolerance, the uniqueness of every person and the greater benefit to all, then this is as it should be.

So instead of throwing up our hands and giving in to those who argue that multiculturalism is a divisive and corrosive force in the context of the nation state, our leaders must work at renewing it. We must turn off the tap of what *The Guardian's* Martin Jacques called "Caucasian superiority". We must work with leaders of ethnic communities to ensure that through leadership the values of tolerance and respect are enhanced in practical ways. Above all, we must ensure that the war on terrorism is not used as an excuse to close our borders to people fleeing hardship and repression.

The diatribes of Le Pen, Fortuyn and Italy's Silvio Berlusconi against Muslims are as morally repugnant and dangerous as Hitler's violent anti-Semitism. Scapegoating and treatment of human beings as somehow inferior (as in not wanting "that type of person here") are totally incompatible with democracy and they breed state-sanctioned violence.

In politics it is easy to preach fear, hatred and intolerance. It is hard yet decent to promote tolerance, togetherness, forgiveness and compassion. But surely leadership is about taking hard decisions. Do we not have almost universal respect for Nelson Mandela precisely because he preached tolerance and forgiveness, not fear and retribution?

Australia and Europe need thousands of Mandelas who stand firm behind the universality of human rights. No comfort should be given to the bigotry and hate that Le Pen and others represent. No apologies or shifts to the hard right in policy should be contemplated if we want to enhance the liberal project.

Why an obsession with sovereignty can harm our security.

Introduction

In the lead up to the creation of the International Criminal Court late last century, the US made it clear that it would not sign up. Was this approach counter-productive? I wrote this article at the turn of the century during that debate.

In the weeks following September 11 many in Western Countries, including a few brave souls in the United States, asked one of the tough questions: Why is it that some people hate the United States so much that they are prepared to die attacking it?

Many feared asking this question as it would bring immediate attacks 'of terrorists sympathies' as if it would not be possible to both ask the question 'why' *and* condemn the attacks.

The attacks of September 11 *were* wrong, and nothing can excuse them. But to not ask what motivates people to undertake these attacks leaves the US open to further strikes – and if Australia is not careful we could become target number two.

A critical analysis of the United States, particularly its foreign policy, rapidly reveals a level of hypocrisy that frustrates, aggravates and intimidates the friends of the United States. To its enemies it adds motivational fuel to the fire driving the hatred of people like bin Laden.

Let us look at just a couple of examples.

The US sees itself as the world policeman defending Human Rights and democracy around the world.

In Vietnam American soldiers, led by Lieutenant Cally, murdered over 150 innocent villagers. Cally was tried, convicted and spent a massive 3 weeks in prison. And the US criticises Indonesia for handing down lenient sentences to the militias responsible for the killings in East Timor.

The US criticises countries like China for detaining dissenters without trial. Yet it detains Al Quaida and Taliban suspects in Cuba without access to legal representation, no trial, no charge and no trial date.

Recently an Australian was detained in Pakistan. He was handed over to the Americans and is now detained in Guantanamo Bay as an Al Quaida suspect. He was not in Afghanistan, did not take part in the September 11 attacks and did not fight with the Taliban. He has no access to a lawyer, no court review, no trial date – nothing.

If it was an objective of the September 11 terrorists to undermine the freedoms, checks and balances of western society, one must now ask if the terrorists have not succeeded. The US is throwing out basic rights like a right to trial and access to lawyers. Yet they still criticise other countries for doing likewise.

Further, the US does not wish to ratify the International Criminal Court Treaty as President Bush says that it will undermine US sovereignty. At the same time the US bombed (rightly) Yugoslavia over the atrocities in Kosovo, regardless of Yugoslavia's sovereignty, bombed Iraq regardless of Iraq's right to fly Iraqi aircraft in Iraq, bombed (erroneously) factories in Sudan, regardless of Sudan's territorial sovereignty.

The US invaded Panama, Grenada, Vietnam, Cambodia, Laos, Afghanistan and helped coup leaders like Pinochet, all regardless of other nation's sovereignty.

The US will not subject itself to a review of an international court at the same time that it demands that Rwanda, Yugoslavia, Bosnia, Croatia and other countries do.

It demanded that Libya should handover the Lockerbie suspects to an international trial, but objected to any questioning of US targeting decisions in bombing mainly civilian objects in Belgrade.

I once found myself sharing a beer with the US Military Attaché to Rwanda. I asked him why the US was so hypocritical in demanding that no-one undermine their sovereignty whilst they bomb so many others in the name of Human Rights.

He said that I did not understand. Enforcing Human Rights was something that you did to everyone else, not the US, as the US had the Bill of Rights.

I suppose that explains slavery, erroneous death penalties, their own war crimes and the wonderful harmonious society that the US is.

But US hypocrisy is not limited to Human Rights; look at their actions in Trade. Tell and Australian sheep farmer that there is no hypocrisy in US trade policy. The US puts quotas on our lamb, and demands the EU stop subsidising theirs.

The US demands free trade, but claims for itself the right to fine Australian companies that trade with Cuba, even if those Australian companies have no presence in the US.

Even though the terrorist attacks on the US were unambiguously wrong, it is hard to reject an argument that anger at US hypocrisy is one of the many motivational factors that the terrorists use. Increased hypocrisy, like the refusal to accept an international review over US military or the International Criminal Court, whilst demanding that other countries be punished, only adds to the hatred.

And now we turn to Australia.

Howard has said that speaking to a congress full of interns, fill-ins and about 50 congressmen and women was the highlight of his political life. We stand side by side with the US in the fight on terror, he says. We do not question the detention of Australian citizens without trial, lawyer or charge by the US.

And now we see that the US is worried about their sovereignty and will not ratify the International Criminal Court Treaty. John Howard says that he understands the 'powerful' arguments of the US and is reviewing our stance. Our sovereignty may be threatened, he says. We may not ratify either.

In the meantime he says we support the US even in attacking Iraq, regardless of their sovereignty.

I ask you, if Australia follows the US line and claims our sovereignty must prevail, but nobody else's can, then are we not guilty of the same hypocrisy? If we are guilty do you think that our national security and safety is being helped or undermined?

Do not get us wrong; to fight terror is a good thing. To fight for Human Rights is a good thing. But to point the finger at others and refuse criticism of us is wrong. It invites criticism and attack, both political and physical.

We can continue to support the US, but we must also reject its hypocrisy. It seems that ratifying the ICC treaty may quickly become our test. To fail to ratify will severely threaten our

National Security because it will invite the same hatred of us as many feel for the US. What is good for the goose is after all good for the gander.

Time for an International Criminal Court.

Introduction

Greg Barns and I lobbied hard for ratification of the International Criminal Court treaty. This article, published originally in the Australian Financial Review, we wrote in 2002.

Twenty-five years ago this week Australia, together with the International Red Cross, took the lead in the development of the law on War Crimes. Yet today our nation has members of its government who wish to turn our back on past achievements and run a populist line of 'national sovereignty'. This will ensure that we lose our status as a country committed to the continued development of laws against War Crimes.

On the 11th of June 1977, over a hundred States adopted two Protocols to the Geneva Conventions. Nations like Australia had pushed successfully for the Law of War to now cover internal conflicts, wars of National Liberation and to give further protection to innocent civilians caught in the cross fire of conflict.

It is breaches of these Protocols and other laws that have Milosevic and the perpetrators of the Rwandan Genocide facing justice in two ad hoc International Courts.

Australia had no difficulty signing up in 1977 as we recognised that the need to bring the world's evil to justice was greater than evil's need to appeal to 'National Sovereignty'. But today we are letting the world's evil off the hook.

We are being asked to ratify the Rome Statute that would create the first permanent International Criminal Court to try the world's evil – and government backbenchers led by former minister Bronwyn Bishop are refusing.

So why are Bishop and her supporters refusing? They claim that the International Criminal Court, with the power to try Australian soldiers, is a threat to our 'National Sovereignty' and not in our 'national interest'. They say that Australia's courts would no longer be the final arbiters of Australian's guilt.

Bishop is not alone in her view. Milosevic, Pinochet, the WWII Japanese Leaders, the Nazis and Pol Pot have all been on record at various times saying that international courts like this should not be supported. So have the Americans – not surprising given their record in places like Vietnam.

Funnily enough though, those taking the opposing view, that the court should go ahead, include the Australian Defence Force, the United Kingdom, Australia's negotiating team at the ICC Conference, most of the Commonwealth, modern day Japan, modern day Germany and funnily enough, modern day Yugoslavia.

Admiral Chris Barrie, Chief of the Australian Defence Force, said that the creation of the ICC would be no threat to Australian forces, rather the Court's existence would make Australian soldiers' jobs easier and safer in peace-keeping operations.

British Foreign Secretary Robin Cook said that Britain has ratified the ICC treaty as "it is in Britain's national interest to do so. A more stable, democratic world is safer to live, travel and trade in."

Each of the above quotes negate arguments put by Bishop and highlight how odd it seems that Australia may side with Milosevic instead of the Australian Defence Force, with the Japanese WWII leaders instead of the Commonwealth or Pol Pot instead of our own negotiating team.

But rather than just make simple comparisons, let's analyse Bishop's argument. Does the treaty threaten or undermine our National Sovereignty, and more importantly, if it does, should it?

The answer to the first question is 'yes to a degree'. If a permanent international court is established, and it has the power to try our soldiers if we do not try them, then our sovereignty is lessened. Bishop is partly right.

But, wait a second, let's look at that a bit more closely.

The ICC will only try Australians that in the future may be accused of Genocide or horrendous crimes if, and only if, Australia refuses to try them in Australia. If an accused Australian soldier is prosecuted in our system, then no sovereignty is lost.

No one can take our soldiers away if we have a go at them first.

This leads on to the second question. If an Australian soldier commits or is suspected of committing a horrendous offence and a future government refuses to prosecute them, should an international court step in?

We said that it should with the Germans. We said that it should with the Japanese. We said that it should with the Rwandans. We said that it should with the Serbs, Croats and Bosnians.

Must we refuse it now? And what of future Rwandas or Bosnias?

So to Bronwyn Bishop, and John Howard, we say 'Yes' you are right. A little sovereignty would be lost with the creation of the International Criminal Court, but only if future governments fail to act against atrocities that future Australian soldiers will hopefully never commit.

But sovereignty in that case not only 'should' be lost but 'must' be lost. If we don't have the guts to prosecute our own people if they commit crime on an horrendous scale, then someone else *must*.

If we do not try our people for War Crimes, then someone should, just as we have been strong advocates of the prosecution of the Japanese, Germans, Rwandans, Bosnians, Croats and Serbs.

Guantanamo shows the USA has learnt nothing from 9/11.

Introduction

Do US double standards help their security? I wrote this article in the mid 2000's. How do we look back in hindsight?

One key way to turn past adversity into future strength is to analyse where things went wrong. US treatment of Taliban and Al Qa'ida fighters in Guantanamo Bay shows that, in part, the US has failed to learn from September 11, and is missing an opportunity to move forward.

From the start it must be made clear that the September 11 attacks on the United States are inexcusable. Even so, we must ask why it is that *so many* people hate the United States *so much,* that people were prepared to die in spectacular suicide attacks in New York.

One answer is the US's approach to international affairs. The US lays down one rule for themselves, and another for all else. For example:

The US is currently holding a number of former Taliban and Al Qa'ida fighters in detention at the Guantanamo Bay military base, denying these fighters the rights accorded to Prisoners of War – never mind the fact that these fighters we taken in the US styled 'War' on terror. Never mind the fact that the US demanded that the USSR grant POW status to Afghan prisoners during the USSR's time in that country.

The United States claims that the fighters held by the US are 'illegal combatants' and not Prisoners of War. They claim that the prisoners were wearing no uniforms at the time of capture and therefore were not 'legal combatants'. Here the US has a technical, yet pedantic, point.

The Third Geneva Convention of 1949 specifies that POW status only applies to those who were combatant members of an organised military force, undertaking military operations, carrying weapons openly and wearing a *fixed and distinctive sign recognisable at a distance*. Clearly Taliban and Al Qa'ida fighters would not technically comply with this definition if they were wearing no uniform, hence the US, if all else was ignored, is correct to deny POW status on that point.

However the story is not that simple.

In 1977 the international community agreed to an Additional Protocol that altered the definition applicable to POWs. The alterations removed the necessity to wear a uniform or carry arms openly. Under the Additional Protocol the Taliban fighters would, and should, clearly be given POW status and protection.

Although over 150 countries have ratified the Protocols, the US has not. They have 'signed' the Protocol but not 'ratified' it; hence it is not law in the US – although by signing the document they indicate an acceptance of the essence of it.

It is now generally accepted practice in international affairs that people acting as part of a military force, when captured, should be treated as POWs regardless of uniforms, gaining prisoners certain rights and imposing on them certain obligations. Recently the US demanded that US prisoners held by Milosevic were to be treated as POWs, even though the US strenuously denied that a 'war' was taking place.

The US has chosen to ignore state practice with respect to the prisoners in Cuba, thumbing their national nose at the world, thereby pretending that state practice applies to all other countries but not themselves.

Many countries are now lining up in criticism of the US, including France, the UK and other western countries. Exception:- Australia, which again tries to act as the loyal deputy of the US.

Similarly, the US refuses to ratify the treaty setting up the proposed International Criminal Court to prosecute War Criminals. The US refuses to accept the proposition that the International Community could prosecute US citizens, while at the same time refuses to allow Taliban and Al Qa'ida fighters access to trials outside the far from neutral US.

The US also strenuously objected to the International Criminal Tribunal for the Former Yugoslavia (ICTY). Cynics wonder whether this was due to reluctance by the US to have some of the questionable targeting decisions undertaken by the US during the Kosovo conflict tested. At the same time, the US pushed for the extension of the ICTY mandate to cover Serbian atrocities in the Kosovo conflict.

Granting POW status to those Taliban and Al Qa'ida fighters held in Cuba would not deny the chance to prosecute individuals for crimes of terrorism. It would send a signal to the world that the US was 'practicing what it preached' in granting universal Human Rights to people under US care, not just demanding that others do.

'Do as I say not as I do' does not work for parents with children, nor does it work in international relations. The US insistence on 'Victors Law' and a continuance of a hypocritical foreign policy approach does not help US security, particularly in the Middle East.

Australia's insistence on following the US does not help ours.

B: Conflict and war.

Did Russia Check-Mate the West in Crimea?

Consider this hypothetical: 60 years ago a dictatorial regime grants territory, let's call it A, from one of its regions, let's call it B, to another we can call C – without any consultation with the people of either A, B or C.

We now have a group A living amongst group C at the stroke of a dictator's pen even though Group A and Group B have closer if not identical ethnic ties, where as Group C sees themselves as different. This is not something the West would support.

Fifty years later the dictator's regime has collapsed. Groups B and C now become different countries. However there remains the historical anachronism of what to do with Group A that had been handed over by the now gone dictator? In haste an agreement is made not to rock the boat. So A stays with C and does not return to B.

Ten years further on the people of A now decide that they wish to return to B. Group A has a referendum to determine their future but C objects to the vote.

Taking personalities and nations out of it one would think that the West would back the self determination of Group A, recognise the past act of a dictator as invalid and put pressure on Group C to allow the return of Group A to the territory of Group B. After all, that would be democratic.

Now lets put names in the circumstances to see how the dynamic changes.

In the 1950's Soviet Dictator Khrushchev takes the largely ethnic Russian region of Crimea from the Russian Republic and hands it to the Ukrainian Republic. No consultation, just a stroke of a pen.

In the 1990's the Soviet Union dissolves. In the mess that follows an agreement is signed that Crimea will remain an autonomous territory under the sovereignty of Ukraine. Most people though still speak Russian and identify with Russian culture more than Ukrainian culture.

The last presidential election in Ukraine elected a pro-Moscow president who tried to reverse the further integration of

Ukraine with Europe and instead look back to Russia. The pro European western part of the country and the pro Russian eastern part of the country are now in dispute.

A 'popular apprising' overthrew the pro-Russian president and replaced him with a pro European interim government. This triggered the push in the autonomous region of Crimea to re-join Russia.

The Crimean parliament officially requested Moscow to accept Crimea back into Russia using the deeply flawed March referendum as justification. Despite the referendum's deep flaws, no serious player disputes the will of the majority of Crimean people is to return to Russia.

While this narrative is a gross simplification, the essential issues are accurate. But so what?

It is true that many in the West don't like Putin or his dogma. Certainly our media carries only the government anti-Russian view. But should Putin bashing be put aside in favour of respecting the genuine will of the people of Crimea?

Some may say that would have been appeasement. But consider the alternative.

If instead of objecting, the West had recognised the will of the Crimean people and the undoing of the dictator's pen stroke, then Crimea could be back in Russia with out a loss of face to the West because the West would have agreed.

There is historical consistency for this. The British agree that Scotland can have a self-determination referendum without Britain voting. Australia pushed for East Timor's freedom without an Indonesian vote. So why does the West argue that all of Ukraine must vote for Crimea's future?

The historical narrative of undoing Khrushchev's pen stroke would 'insulate' Crimea from becoming a historical precedent to apply worldwide. The Ukrainians would have a face saving way of losing territory and the West could have avoided a confrontation with Russia that ultimately Russia will win.

But yet again personalities seem to undermine genuine chances of peaceful transfers and what do we have?

The West has waived the collective finger at Putin. Putin has ignored them and used 'democracy' as one of his arguments. The only way the Can now win is if Putin withdraws because of sanctions, or is forced out by military action. Sanctions won't do that and the West will not invade.

Putin has check-mated the West. The consequence of such a visible loss by the west is yet to fully play out. But it is a loss that did not have to happen if only the will of the people of Crimea had been accepted and respected.

Is the west getting policy on Egypt wrong?

Images of protests in Cairo's Tahrir Square have flashed across TV screens in Australia, UK, US and all around the world. Images of a deposed dictator in court, a new democratically elected Islamic president subsequently overthrown by street protests and armoured vehicles, also ends up in court.

A military leader now says he may run for president in new elections due by mid-April, but only after he banned the last president's party, the Muslim Brotherhood. 'They are terrorists' cried the head of the military General (now Field Marshal) el-Sisi.

The US and UK disagree.

Yes Egypt is in a mess. But does it matter anyway? And if it does, has the West got the policy settings right or are Western governments fanning flames on a fire it does not understand?

Less than four years ago an Arab Spring arose toppling dictators and heralding a new hope in North Africa. Tunisia, Libya and Egypt all saw long-term dictators fall. Elections brought new leaders to power.

'All hail the great elections' cried the US as a secular dictator in Egypt was replaced by an Islamic party that many feared would steer Egypt away from secularism towards fanaticism.

The West's citizenry often lament the short term thinking of Western politicians. Driven by electoral cycles western politicians look for trends measured in sound bites, months or years. Long-term historical perspective is not something the West is well known for.

No wonder the West is all confused about Egypt. Egypt can only be viewed through a complicated and long-term historical prism. It is too complex for headlines. To difficult for Western politicians perhaps?

I spoke to many people on a recent visit to Egypt. The average Egyptian will tell you that theirs is a history of both religious tolerance and religious change. Normal people in the street would explain current events within a long-term historical narrative missing in the west. Their narrative runs as follows:

Over 4,000 years ago the pharaohs built the pyramids and temples in honour of their gods. On these temple walls are carved great depictions, including the god Isis breast-feeding her son, the god Horace.

When Alexander the Great invaded around 300 BC adopted the local religion rather than imposing one. In his temples there are carvings of Isis breast-feeding not Horace, but Alexander - a self styled king-god who adapted to Egyptian ways.

When the Romans persecuted Jewish families around the time of Christ, Jewish families fled for Cairo. Mary, Joseph and Jesus himself sought refuge. Their hiding place is still preserved in Cairo.

When Constantine the Great adopted Christianity for all the empire including Egypt in around 300 AD, the Coptic Christian Church would, like the temples of earlier years, paint depictions of Mary breast-feeding Christ in almost exactly the same manner as Isis feeding Horace, and Isis feeding Alexander.

Emperor Julian in the early 300's broke with tradition and imposed Christianity with no tolerance to other religions. It was break with tradition that did not last long.

When Islam came to dominate Egypt in the mid 600's the Coptic Christian Church and Islamic rulers agreed on a cohabitation that included the Jews. Indeed Egyptians will tell you that until the foundation of Israel, there were no issues between Jews and Egyptians.

While the above is an historical over-simplification and may well gloss over many atrocities, it does represent a self-belief that many Egyptians hold. There is a self image that they are a religiously tolerant society.

And then came President Morsi.

In barely more than a year of Morsi's rule over 70 churches were said to be destroyed. Increased Islamification was disrupting society. Secularist Egyptians became restless. Rumours spread within Egyptian society that Morsi himself had approved the foundation of new Al-Quaida training bases in the Sainai.

The Germans found evidence of Morsi's collusion with Al Quaida but could not blow the whistle too loudly. The Germans were objecting to the American tapping of the German Chancellor's phone, just as the Germans were tapping the Egyptian President's one.

Under Morsi the government was threatening the Egyptian self-image of religious tolerance. Approximately 23 million, nearly a third of the country's population, came out in protest and were supported by the military.

Was this a protest a popular uprising, or was it a coup? Does it matter?

The US declared the action a coup and suspended military aid– including the support the Egyptian Army needed to fight the Al-Quaida bases in the Sanai.

But was the US right? When is a coup a 'coup' and when is it a legitimate expression of democratic will?

To US, UK and Australian eyes, the only legitimate democratic process is through the ballot box. If you get a government you don't like, you just have to wait for the next election.

But what of a new democracy where a newly elected government does not do as it promised? Should the population sit back and wait for the next election as the fundamental nature and tenant of their society is threatened, or is it democratic to rise up - even with the support of the Army?

Backing the Arab Spring was important, however cementing the gains will be much harder and much more difficult. Getting the next step right is more important for long-term international stability. The West in danger of insisting that democracy can only be exercised through the ballot box and perhaps is missing the point that some democracies have a rocky start.

After all, didn't the US have both a revolutionary war and a civil war?

Iraq: The West's Moral Dilemma

Introduction

In the lead up to the Iraq war, it was very easy to say 'no blood for oil'. It is very easy to say 'I prefer peace'. But would keeping Saddam Hussein in power really have been better? Would that really have been 'peace'?

While this was published before the war, in hindsight would the opinion express be different? Maybe not – but in hindsight, the poor post war occupation makes it is a view certainly more difficult to sustain.

Multimedia (ebook only)
This article was first published in The Age on 3rd February 2003, here.

In 1994, during the height of the Bosnian conflict, aid workers often faced a staggering moral dilemma - and this story is true.

Local militia (of ethnic group one) would approach an aid worker and say: "See that village down there (full of ethnic group two)? Well, we are going to 'ethnic cleanse' it. Will you bus the people out, please?"

The aid worker could succumb to the request, become the tool of ethnic cleansing, lose the neutral status of the aid organisation in the eyes of ethnic group two and, consequently, be refused access to other areas where populations may die through lack of food and other aid. This is not a good choice.

Or, on the other hand, the aid worker could refuse to bus the people out. The result would be an immediate attack on the village and the aid worker would watch perhaps hundreds of people die. This is not a good choice either.

And here lies the heart of a moral dilemma. In the case given above, one may be tempted to search for another answer. One may say: "Well, we could ask for intervention, or consult colleagues, or try diplomacy, or . . ."

But this ignores the fact that a decision had to be made immediately. To make no decision - that is, to say "I need to consult" or "Can I tell you later?" - would be met with: "I have no time, I'm attacking now."

With this real dilemma there is no "better option" to choose. The aid worker has two, and only two, choices: bus the people out and thousands of others may die later, or don't bus the people out and watch hundreds die.

No matter how much one may like to have another option, no matter how many better choices one can create in theory, fact reveals only two options - and on several occasions young delegates of aid organisations had to choose not the best but the "least bad" option. Young delegates had to choose who would die.

We are now faced with a global moral dilemma of a similar type.

Many of those who do not support intervention in Iraq argue that the human cost of intervention is too high - yet they ignore the human cost of non-intervention. No one outside Iraq denies that Saddam Hussein is a tyrant. No one denies that he continues to torture, murder and use rape as a tool of control.

For example, Saddam has a systematic plan to eradicate the Ma'dan, or so-called Marsh Arabs. Human Rights Watch estimates that the population of Marsh Arabs has dropped from 250,000 to 40,000 in just 15 years (see www.hrw.org). That is 210,000 real people dead or missing. This is on top of an estimated 100,000 Kurds who have suffered the same fate. This is on top of the countless numbers who are members of ethnic groups, political organisations and normal members of Iraqi society who have suffered at Saddam's hand without any international attention.

Added to this is the repression, rape, torture, amputations and branding that are part of the Iraqi system of "justice".

The eradication of Marsh Arabs, the repression of Kurds, the continued rape, murder and torture - this is the cost of non-intervention.

If the United Nations, the United States and Australia have the power to stop this, yet we do not, are we not then to some degree morally responsible for the activity?

Some say: "Well, the US helped create Saddam!" - as if that is a reason to not intervene now. Some say: "The US only wants to change the regime to get their hands on Iraqi oil" - as if preventing the US from doing so is reason enough to allow rape, torture and killings to continue. Some say: "There has to be another way" - as if that had not been attempted for the past 12 years.

The fact is, we have a moral dilemma. Like the aid worker in Bosnia, we are searching for a "third option", a better way. Like the aid worker, we are slowly coming to the realisation that there is no third option.

To say "continue with diplomacy" is to say "continue with rape, murder and torture". To say "it is not our problem" is to say "continue with rape, murder and torture". To say "the US is a global imperialist that just wants to control the oil" is to say "continue with rape, murder and torture". Anything except regime change is to say "continue with rape, murder and torture".

In 1994, the world had advance warning of the Rwandan genocide. The world, Australia included, ignored the pleas of General Delaire, the UN force commander, when he asked for a mere 2500 soldiers to stop genocide from happening.

The world said "this is not our war" and refused the request. Just 100 days later, up to one million people were dead. That is 10,000 a day, every day, for 100 days. That was the cost of non-intervention.

In 1992, the Europeans (especially the French and the Germans) said to the US that Bosnia was a European problem and that the US should keep out. "We will fix it," they said. For three years, the Europeans tried and failed and 250,000 people died before the US intervened. That was the cost of non-intervention.

I find it interesting that many of the people who oppose US intervention in Iraq also believe that human rights are more important than national sovereignty. But if diplomacy and sanctions fail, how else do you support human rights if not through the use of force?

At an anti-war rally in Melbourne last week, federal Labor MP Carmen Lawrence said she had heard no "talk of the Iraqi lives that would be obliterated, the inevitable legacy of disability, homelessness and the stream of refugees that would result from attacking Iraq . . . We are invited to deny our shared humanity with the people of Iraq".

But doesn't her argument apply equally to the cost of non-intervention?

40

The US is far from perfect. But we have no "perfect" world policeman. If we want human rights to be enforced, then it has to be with US help. There is no "third option" here, just as there was no third option in Rwanda and Bosnia.

There should be intervention in Iraq for regime change and the UN Security Council should back this, because the cost of non-intervention is just too high.

If the Security Council does not support intervention, then the equation changes and we have another "moral dilemma", don't we?

Iraq, Still the Moral Dilemma

A little over 10 years ago, on the eve of the Iraq war, I wrote on the pages of the Fairfax Press that Iraq was the West's moral dilemma

(see here). I argued that the west had to choose between the least bad of bad options and argued:

"To say "continue with diplomacy" is to say "continue with rape, murder and torture". To say "it is not our problem" is to say "continue with rape, murder and torture". To say "the US is a global imperialist that just wants to control the oil" is to say "continue with rape, murder and torture". Anything except regime change is to say "continue with rape, murder and torture".

Ten years on and views on the Iraq war have hardened in many people's eyes. For most people the issue is black or white – right or wrong, and there is very little grey in public discussion.

Iraq fills our TV screens with violence and mayhem. Last week's bombs in Baghdad reinforce the view that the security situation in Iraq is terrible. But allow me to put a refined view.

I recently visited Iraq and have seen that far from being black and white, Iraq today is as complicated as ever. It is still a moral dilemma and does not lend itself to definitive statements that the war was either definitively right, or definitively wrong.

Australian travellers like me are often asked by people in other countries 'what is the weather like in Australia?' There is a wildly different depending where in Australia you are. North is hot, South is cold.

Likewise asking 'how is the security in Iraq?' encourages an equally broad range of answers, with many regions off limits for non-military travellers. The world cannot even agree on how many innocent people died in the war, with figures reaching from the ludicrously low to the ludicrously high.

For me the anti-war group 'Iraqi Body Count' seems to have worked as hard as anyone to get as accurate data as possible and claim in the range of 112,000-123,000 needless deaths in the decade long war and aftermath. This is as good a starting point as any for understanding the cost of the war.

What about the cost of 'no war'?

In the decade before the war Hussain was estimated by Human Rights Watch and Amnesty International to have killed somewhere between 500,000 and 1 million people.

Can one assume a radical change in Saddam's approach if there were no intervention and the consequent continuation of the Saddam Regime? Can one assume that Saddam would magically have changes, or would it have been a safer assumption to say his brutal regime would have continued?

Can one say that the cost of 'no war' would have been Saddam killing at least 500,000 people?

That is one heck of a moral dilemma to set up where non-intervention kills more innocent people than intervention.

My recent visit though took me out of the world of theoretical numbers and into the world of real people. While many parts of Iraq are off limits to the non-military travel, there is one region of safety, tranquillity and enormous interest. Iraqi Kurdistan.

Iraqi Kurdistan is a part of Iraq you can – and maybe should – visit. For those who did not support the US led war, perhaps a quick tourism visit to a safe region is a better contribution to the country, its people and its economy than tax payers' dollars than complaining about George Bush's war?

What is more, most nationalities can obtain a visa on arrival in Erbil after the short two and a half hour flight from Dubai. So visiting Iraq on a two or three day stop over on Qantas' new Kangaroo Route to Europe via Dubai is quite possible.

That is a bizarre thought: A stop-over in Iraq on the way to Europe? But is it really safe?

From Erbil, north of Baghdad (Kurdistan's regional capital) to the Turkish border, there is a region steeped in history, wonderful nature, friendly people, economic growth and around a decade of peace and security.

In 1991 following Gulf War 1, Iraqi Kurds, who had been brutally repressed under the Saddam Hussein regime, had hopes of independence supported by the Coalition forces. A rapid withdrawal of the Coalition following the cease-fire gave Hussein freedom to continue repression, until effective autonomy was created by the United Nations no fly zone.

The Kurds themselves then fell into a decade long civil war pitting different factions against each other until Kurdish peace was established in the early 2000's. In 2005 the Kurdish autonomy was recognised in the Iraqi Constitution hence now the Kurds have their own parliament, their own president, and their own armed forces and with their own passport control, issue their own passport stamps. Since then it has been peaceful.

On a spring day Erbil's central square is a bustling place of small coffee shops, hookah-pipes bubbling the sweet scent of apple, families, children and fountains. Friendly and engaging locals will seek to engage in a part Arabic, part English, part Kurdish discussion on geopolitics that will at least result in lots of good coffee being had and new friendships formed.

The Kurds will tell you that they may be no fans of George Bush, but they were brutally repressed by Hussain. There is a strong recognition that their current freedom comes at huge expense to those elsewhere in the country. The discussions around coffee and bubbling hookah pipes shine a new light on the moral dilemmas of the war.

Discussions show that there are winners as well as losers from the Iraq conflict. The winners were not just oil companies. Many of the winners are normal, innocent people like you and me, in this case the Kurds. Discussions in these coffee shops will move any person who has a black-or-white, war-was-right-or-wrong view, to one full of a lot more subtlety and grey.

Another example of the moral dilemma can be found in Erbil's Sami Abdul-Rahman Park. This magnificent, huge and sprawling park is a welcome escape into greenery. Fountains, lakes, flower beds and acres of mown grass are all built over what was the headquarters of Saddam's feared Fifth Corps, that for so long was the brutal instrument of Kurdish repression.

The Kurdish people have only been able to build this island of tranquillity because Saddam Hussein was removed from power. The park was only competed after Saddam was captured and executed. If there had been no intervention in Iraq, Saddam would still have been in power and the 2005 Constitutional Autonomy for the Kurds would not have existed. The repression would have continued and this great park would still have been an army barracks.

But the dilemma is that Iraq is not just a story of the Kurds. We still see the mess that is Baghdad and central Iraq. Although gun violence in Iraq is now lower than in the US – even on a per capita basis – violence continues in Baghdad and surrounding areas. Peace may have come to the Kurds, but it did not come elsewhere.

A war many people did not support has given at least part of Iraq a great future. It left other areas stained with blood. It is hard to stand in Kurdistan and not support the war and the peace it has brought. Likewise, it is hard to stand in Baghdad and support the intervention in Iraq.

But one has to choose. Support for war, supports the Kurds. Condemning Bush, likewise condemns the Kurds. One can't have both outcomes. The moral dilemma continues.

What of North Korea?

Introduction

I travelled to North Korea in February 2013. It was a trip that coincided with the country's third nuclear test.

What is behind that fortress state? These are my impressions.

Multimedia (ebook only)

An edited version of this article was first published in The Independent on 10 March 2013 *here*. There is a video of the journey available *here* and photo gallery *here*.

The cold, unheated concrete bunker heralded our arrival into Democratic People's Republic of Korea (DPRK – North Korea). It looked something out of a World War 2 airfield, and I guessed it was probably built shortly after the Korean War. Bad guess. Construction year: 2010. Oh dear!

Expecting a grilling at immigration, I was surprised how quickly a tall, slim, rather attractive border guard stamped my visa. No questions asked – literally. I really wanted her to ask something. Her eyes wanted me to start up a conversation – or so I told myself.

'What would be my opening line?' I wondered? 'Can I have your mobile number?'

No, that wouldn't work –DPRK has a mobile network but with no access to the international system, unless they are elite.

I moved beyond immigration to the luggage belt. Stopping only once, for a brief electricity cut, the belt barely slowed my arrival to customs. I had three cameras, one video camera and a laptop. I held a concern that the official would not believe my declaration that 'I was not a journalist'. Surprisingly customs took no interests in the camera gear but did register my iPad mini and iPhone. Steve jobs would be impressed. He is officially a threat to the state.

I told myself the few cars on the road must have been due to the Lunar New Year holiday. On leaving Beijing at departure that morning the roads were also deserted. In the 48 hours before I left

China's capital two million people had left returning home to their families for Chinese New Year.

Surprised, I was, over the next five days to find that the sparse roads outside of the airport were the busiest of the trip. A new expression has now entered my lexicon; the Pyongyang traffic jam – meaning an empty road.

The westerner in me automatically saw this as a criticism. No cars equates to no wealth. Yet everything has multiple perspectives. No cars means no traffic and no delays. No cars means no pollution. In how many developing countries' capital cities can you take a lung full of air and think 'ah, that is clean'?

The North Korean capital also lacks Coke, McDonalds and KFC signs, but did have the odd propaganda poster with words I didn't understand. Never mind, the anti-American message comes through clearly in the pictures.

We arrived at the hotel just before dinner. Our group was split over just two of the 47 potentially available floors. Each other floor stubbornly and suspiciously remained black when viewed from the car park. No lights on any other floor. Perhaps only two floors were operational?

After dinner the night view of the Pyongyang skyline was dark, dotted by a few lonely light bulbs. The odd car on empty roads showed this is not the wealthy country that North Korea's internal propaganda might suggest.

Our guide told us that the government of the DPRK, in the interests of everyone's health, encourages people to walk or cycle, and hence the lack of cars. Even at night. Even below zero.

A visit to the hotel's pool and sauna facility brought me into contact with a few of the local elite permitted to use the facility. Elite or not, the nakedness of Asian style wash areas makes it hard for one to think of a naked change room colleague as an enemy in a deadly game of good and evil.

Day two started with a visit to 'the' Mausoleum. Both Kim Il-sung and Kim Jong-il lie in state in the former office of DPRK's founder Kim Il-sung. 'Office' is a term to be used loosely. Palace, bastion, fortress or grand demonstration of the inequality of a dictatorship, might be a better description.

While the country starved through famines, the Kims lived in acres of marble, lit by millions of dollars' worth of chandeliers. The rich irony is that the masses are now permitted to queue up and enter this grand palace to pay respects to the two leader's embalmed bodies. The masses feel grateful to be allowed in to the previously forbidden building and somehow don't get angry at the juxtaposition of the living environments. On questioning our guides, they didn't seem to even see the juxtaposition, let alone feel angry about it.

There is detailed ritual around being allowed to lay eyes on the 'great' leaders. Bowing three times I circled clockwise around the bodies held in their glass sarcophagi. Like Ho Chi Min and Lenin, the two Kims looked more wax than human, begging the question why only communist countries do this to their dead leaders. Perhaps democracies throw their leaders out and by definition have no desire to lay their eyes on embalmed corpses into the future.

All of the rituals, the marble and palaces, could somehow be anticipated. I did not anticipate the gentle sobbing of people who looked upon their departed leaders. Was the sobbing and emotion real? Undoubtedly, in my view, yes.

Having lived in Yugoslavia under Milosevic and spoken with Islamic extremists in Pakistan, I have come to accept, although I may not agree with them, that people who receive only one source of information, believe that single source of information. Humans, when lacking competing information, tend to accept what they are told by those in authority – particularly if they have been through an education system that does not teach independent thought.

Most North Koreans will have been brought up on a diet of propaganda extolling the semi divine nature of the Kims. If you had been brought up on that diet, and had believed the rituals of the semi divine, you would sob in the presence of their bodies too.

If you are in doubt then think of this: One large group of people across the world believe a man died on the cross only to rise again three days later. Others believe in the God of Abraham, but not in Jesus. Others believe the Prophet Mohammad had the direct word of God flow through his fingers. At least two of those three MUST be wrong – yet around the world in highly educated countries, people believe in those, or other religions with deep passion and sob, flagellate and show deep emotion in rituals of these beliefs handed down over generations.

Religion is a better analogy for the Kims than politics. The personality cult and propaganda around the Kims is more like a religion than mere political control. This is why a free media is more important than a free election as a foundation of democracy. Elections mean nothing if there is no real and informed alternative from which to choose. It becomes a mere exercise in ticking boxes. To have an election, one must have a choice. Hence building a civil society must be a precondition before elections.

Exiting the great hypocrisy of the mausoleum, but before heading to the De Militarized Zone (DMZ), we were taken to various monuments and statues to the Kims that dominate all areas of Pyongyang. Perhaps there is another new expression for the lexicon. North Korea does not have monuments; it has 'Kimuments'. It doesn't have memorials; it has 'Kimorials'.

A short trip on the subway followed, which our official guides declared to be well decorated with art. Clean, efficient, quick and well used by many local people, who tried desperately not to make eye contact with the foreigners and were nervous of our presence. Well decorated and clean, yes, but art – no. Propaganda – yes.

Later in the afternoon we left Pyongyang and headed south towards the DMZ, through another 'Pyongyang traffic jam' of deserted highways. Beautiful landscape, powdered with snow and dotted with powerless, carless, freezing villages with no sign of fun and little life, passed before our eyes as our bus headed south on this, the lunar new year's day.

We started to chat more casually with our guides.

"How much do cars cost here?" one of the group asked.

A bewildered look from the guide and a pause for thought. "Cost?" he asked. "Well, the state gives them", he said with bewilderment on his face.

'Who would buy a car?' he must have been thinking.

This is the real reason that so few cars are on the road. Successful sportspeople, artists, actors or senior bureaucrats are given a car as their reward. It is not possible for normal people to buy them even if they had the money. So much for lack of cars as a means to keep people fit – they just can't be bought.

The further south we headed, the more obvious the military defences became. We were told not to photograph out the windows by guides who are ignorant of Google Earth and that all these things are quite readily visible to anyone on the planet with an internet connection – i.e. not North Koreans.

We stopped for the night in Kaesong using a friendly, hospitable hotel, with sporadic power and a promise of hot water from 7:15 the next morning.

Traditional under floor heating in the rooms and paper doors – not paper thin doors but paper doors like those you would have expected in Tokyo before the great fire – welcomed us. While atmospheric, the paper wall gave the under floor heating a great challenge given that it was minus something cold outside.

The next morning, as my breath condensed in the air and the faded orange glow struggled in the light bulb, I imagined the warm shower.

Alas, the hot water pipe was 'broken', so we were given a bucket of warm water to wash in, followed by breakfast and a visit to the De-Militarized Zone (DMZ).

Four kilometres separates the North and South across the armistice zone said to be one of the most heavily armed zones in the world. Kashmir, Golan, DMZ; three areas competing for an honour no-one should want.

Whilst it was predictable to hear a lot of anti-American rhetoric, some of which might be true and much of which was probably not, there was no mention of South Korea. The two enemies to North Korea seemed to be Japan, prior to WW2, and the United States after WW2. It was also the first time I heard that it was the Russians who defeated Japan in WW2! My guide was genuinely surprised when I told him how many Australians died at the hands of the Japanese and that we all fought on the same side in 1939-1945.

At the end of the DMZ tour I pulled aside our additional military DMZ guide – a Colonel, and told him of my military past.

"Soldier to soldier, we all want peace" I said. He smiled, stepped back and we swapped salutes.

"I don't want to write any more letters to mothers telling them why their son died needlessly", a Filipino General once told me in Mindanao. Like that general I spoke with in Southern Philippines, desperate for his government to find a peaceful solution to the fighting in that province, this North Korean Colonel was training for a war he hoped he would never see. Few professional soldiers want war, but all will respond if their political leaders order it.

For lunch we stopped at a local café. Outside, local kids were taking up the new fad of roller blading. We were permitted to photograph in this tightly controlled space. Strong faces desperately trying to avoid our eyes fled from cameras, lest they be snapped. Every now and again a brave soul would smile back or risk a wave. A few small children waved back. They were quickly grabbed by parents yet to give the anti-fraternisation lesson normally learnt sitting on parental knees.

Under all the reservation and fear, one gets the feeling that somehow the people still want to reach over and say hello. There is friendliness here, desperate to come out but held tightly inside by indoctrination.

We headed to the Myohyangsan for an overnight stay, dinner, exposure to great northern scenery and a new take on the personality cult slowly turning into a religion. We arrived in a grand hotel with freezing cold common areas and mercifully effective under floor hearting in individual rooms. Hot water was put on for an hour before dinner. I showered and dressed, ensuring my thermals were on for the unheated dining room. I'm sure the great leader needs not his thermals at dinner.

Quick to jump out of bed in time for the 7:30 hot water, I bumped my knee into the chair barely illuminated by the flickering orange glow of the bulb struggling for life. Exiting from the shower the day awoke outside my window.

Fine powdered snow, a beautiful lake and lovely mountains filled my window. Nature still knows what she is doing here. Ignoring the politics for a second, North Korea is a spectacularly beautiful country with magnificent mountains, streams and lakes. If not for the politics, North Korea would surely be a favourite tourist destination.

Our first destination for the day was the 'gift house'. It was an opulent, marble encrusted, chandelier filled multi-million dollar building constructed for no other purpose than to show all the gifts given by visiting national or business delegations to leaders of North Korea. For some reason this made me more upset than anything else I had seen.

Two things wounded me. The first was the opulence of the place which has to be considered a waste when looking at alternative uses for the spending such as health, education, electricity or water. The second was the propaganda effect. Our guides were telling us that these gifts were all demonstrations of how much the world respected their leaders and how people from all around the planet came to shower the dictators in gifts, as if it were three kings coming to a baby in a manger.

The lying and the deliberate misrepresentation of the gifts from my country really annoyed me. Australia was counted among the 183 countries that had given a gift to Korea. However, I did not accept the Australian Socialist Party, whoever they are, as true representatives of Australia. Here, in the 'gift house', the DPRK was lying about my country. They were lying about me! This was now personal.

Near the end of the day we were given the news that the Democratic People's Republic of Korea had undertaken their third nuclear test. Discussion on the bus back to Pyongyang ensued.

I recall a conversation I had with a group of 20-somethings in Teheran some years earlier. For those young men and women the capacity for Iran to have nuclear technology was a point of pride. It was also, for them, a point of fairness. If others have nuclear weapons and power, why couldn't they?

For our North Korean guides, the conversation started a similar way, except that our group included Belgians, Finns, Norwegians and me, an Australian. We also had two Americans. One was big, strong and silent. The other was younger and had not yet learnt that the best form of American communication is subtlety.

After the initial spiel around national pride and fairness, the Scandinavians and I put our view that our countries could have developed nuclear weapons but chose not to. We saw it as a sign of strength to not develop the weapons. As nationals of countries that all had the technology to develop nuclear weapons but chose not to, we lent strength to our argument that nuclear testing was a bad idea. We also launched a strong defence of the Non-Proliferation Treaty.

In the same way I pointed out that Australia had led in rocket technology in the 1950s, but stopped developing the technology and used money for health and education instead. Perhaps the DPRK could take that choice too?

"But what about the Americans?" Our guides legitimately ask.

The Europeans in our group launched a strong critique of US foreign policy. More than anything else this critique had our guides thinking these foreigners were not patsies for American foreign policy. Instead, by launching a harsh critique of the United States, the Europeans lent strength to their other arguments against North Korean testing. Perhaps this would have our guides thinking a little.

Day five started with toast and breakfast in conversation about the nuclear tests announced the day before. We then headed to the study house, where Pyongyang youth went for post-curricular studies, and perhaps the most clever bit of North Korean propaganda.

We were shown the study hall were students were allowed to access the internet – or so we were told. A quick look at IE 7's set up showed access to a Local Area Network with pre-saved sites mainly in Korean. Students were told that the computers were accessing the internet. No longer did they have to complain of lack of access. What these students didn't know was that they were accessing a complete fraud of pre-saved sites held in a central server. Very, very clever control by the authorities.

The Study House was another palatial, marble filled but freezing cold monumental construction. The cold gave us yet another phrase. Pyongyang central heating: when you need hat, gloves and coat inside.

It wasn't until we got to the railway museum, where mentions of the 'Great Leader's' name outnumbered mentions of words such as 'train', 'railway' and 'track', that we twigged. A railway museum is not a museum of railways. It is a museum about Kim

Il-sung's 'heroic and patriotic' role in railways. Likewise the Heavy Industry Museum was not about heavy industry. It was a museum to the 'Great Leader's' role in heavy industry. The museums are in fact a test of the cult of personality, not museums.

The cult of personality is all pervasive, invasive, evil, but very, very clever.

Day six saw our train ride back to China. As the train crossed the border we sighed a breath of relief to be welcomed back to the comparative freedom offered by the People's Republic of China. We would now get the internet, but not Facebook! The comparative freedom we immediately felt crossing into China tells us more about North Korea than it does about the Asian giant.

On the train the whole group started to digest what the trip to the Democratic People's Republic of Korea really meant to them. For each person it would be slightly different but similar.

At the end of the day for me the trip is more about people than monuments and buildings. One of our guides, a 28-year-old, intelligent young woman, clearly loved the country and her people. She was a normal person like the rest of us. She wondered who she would marry, how many children she would have and what the future would hold for those children. She was no different from most 28-year-old single females anywhere in the world.

I would have liked to have stayed in touch with her and seen what the future brought her and perhaps the family she wanted to have. This question of how to stay in touch demonstrates that divide the politics and leadership places between us, or any other people from within and outside the DPRK.

The way I live my life, with constant travel, makes it very hard to send me an old-fashioned physical letter. I travel too much to risk posting a postcard or a letter that may never find me. I rely on email and social networks. But there is no internet in North Korea. There is no option for a North Korean to stay in touch by electronic means.

So here we have it, two potential friends reaching across political and cultural divides, separated by politics with no way of being able to stay in touch.

North Korea: the battle is between governments and not people.

President Kim has said it is now time to deal with the 'American problem' once and for all. He claims he now has the capacity to not only attack the United States, but he claims the capacity to win.

Tension on the Korean Peninsular have come to the point where a truly horrific war could take place.

Many are looking for the real motivations. Almost certainly there are other agendas at play. Complicated issues of foreign policy rarely have simple solutions. However, more frighteningly, perhaps Kim believes what he is saying. The world is far more dangerous if North Korean officials believe they can win.

On my recent visit to North Korea I saw two things: Firstly, the degree of self-delusion is all pervasive such that an inflated self-belief is real. Secondly, of war comes to pass, it is normal people that will suffer, and normal North Koreans are not too different from all of us.

But how could self-delusion reach such a grand scale that North Korean officials or people could believe they could successfully take on the United States?

North Koreans have been brought up on a diet of propaganda extolling the semi divine nature of the three president Kims. Both Kim Il-sung and Kim Jong-il lie in state in the former office of DPRK's founder Kim Il-sung.

'Office' is a term to be used loosely. Palace, bastion, fortress or grand demonstration of the inequality of a dictatorship, might be a better description.

While the country starved through famines, the Kims lived in acres of marble, lit by millions of dollars' worth of chandeliers. The rich irony is that the masses are now permitted to queue up and enter this grand palace to pay sobbing respects to the two leader's embalmed bodies. The masses feel grateful to be allowed in to the previously forbidden building and somehow don't get angry at the juxtaposition of the living environments. On questioning our guides, they didn't seem to even see the juxtaposition, let alone feel angry about it.

All of the marble and chandeliers could somehow be anticipated. I did not anticipate the gentle sobbing of people who looked upon their departed leaders. Was the sobbing and emotion real? Undoubtedly, in my view, yes.

Having lived in Yugoslavia under Milosevic and spoken with Islamic extremists in Pakistan, I have come to accept, although I may not agree with them, that people who receive only one source of information, believe that single source of information. Humans, when lacking competing information, tend to accept what they are told by those in authority – particularly if they have been through an education system that does not teach independent thought.

North Koreans have but one source of information from cradle to grave – and that source is the State. The State tells them their leaders are semi-divine. They have even reset the calendar. The year is the year 103 AK. It is 103 years since the first Kim's birth.

The State tells the people that the government of the DPRK, in the interests of everyone's health, encourages people to walk or cycle, and hence the lack of cars. Even at night. Even below zero. This was an early reminder of mass indoctrination. Hence why there are few cars.

The State says the country is in good shape. The State says that nuclear weapons are a good thing.

The State says that in a war against America, North Korea would win.

Normal people believe what the State says because they have no alternative source of information. No internet, not international media, few tourists coming to whisper quiet words in North Korean ears.

If you had been brought up such a diet, believing the rituals of the semi divine, sobbing in the presence of their bodies, you might believe North Korea could win too.

Religion is a better analogy for the Kims than politics. The personality cult and propaganda around the Kims is more like a religion than mere political control. Many believe in the words of Abraham, other Mohammed (PBUH) and others Jesus Christ. Not all three can be right. Believe is subjective.

The west would be foolish to make policy assuming that the North Koreans do not believe in their own strength. Some senior people may know the truth, but most will believe the propaganda and perception is reality when it comes to motivating populations – even when the population is full of people have simple and normal hopes and desires similar to ours.

One of my guides, a 28-year-old, intelligent young woman, clearly loved the country and her people. She wondered who she would marry, how many children she would have and what the future would hold for those children. She was no different from most 28-year-old single females anywhere in the world.

If countries go to war, it is people like her who would suffer.

I would have liked to have stayed in touch with her and seen what the future brought her and perhaps the family she wanted to have. This question of how to stay in touch demonstrates that divide the politics and leadership places between us as people.

I rely on email and social networks. But there is no internet in North Korea. There is no option for a North Korean to stay in touch by electronic means.

So here we have it, two potential friends reaching across political and cultural divides, separated by politics and possible conflict with no way of being able to stay in touch.

So when reading about the nuclear tests I would say this: the regime that runs North Korea is evil and megalomaniacal. But the people are normal. They are like us. They want the best for their children, but they have been indoctrinated.

We may disagree with the leaders, but let's also remember the people, and how hard it is for just to stay in touch with people who are just normal souls, like us.

The Iraq shadow should not stop intervention in Syria.

I have an on-going decade long dispute with my step-mother. She thinks the invasion of Iraq was a bad thing and that the Iraqis should have been left alone to sort out their own problems. Perhaps, the theory goes, they would have found a peaceful way to overthrow Saddam. Such a peaceful overthrow would have been better than war.

Her argument suggests that Syrians should now be given the chance to prove the possibility of freeing themselves without foreign intervention. More likely though, Syria now provides the terrible alternative that would have befallen Iraqis should Saddam have stayed in power.

We had the same disagreement when a little over 10 years ago, on the eve of the Iraq war, I wrote of the moral dilemma around Iraq in the pages of the Fairfax Press (see here). I argued that there were no good options leaving the west to choose between the 'least bad' of bad options. I wrote:

"To say "continue with diplomacy" is to say "continue with rape, murder and torture". To say "it is not our problem" is to say "continue with rape, murder and torture". To say "the US is a global imperialist that just wants to control the oil" is to say "continue with rape, murder and torture". Anything except regime change is to say "continue with rape, murder and torture".

Like Iraq of a decade ago, today's constant re-examinations of movable 'red lines', searches for diplomatic solutions and consequent inaction over Syria allows the continuation of rape, murder, torture. Unlike Iraq, where there were no Weapons of Mass Destruction stockpiles found, more evidence of real WMD usage in Syria is being seen with chemicals similar to those Saddam used against the Kurds in Fallujah.

Even with the horror we see on today's TV screens, how do we take the lesson Iraq gives us? Is it a warning of why the west should not intervene despite the mounting Syrian death toll? Conventional wisdom says Iraq is still a basket case after a botched US occupation that was clearly unjustifiable in hindsight?

Recently I visited Iraq and have seen that far from being black and white, Iraq today is as complicated as ever. It is still a moral dilemma and does not lend itself to definitive statements that the war was either definitively right, or definitively wrong.

While one can point to areas around Baghdad as being enormously insecure, great swathes of northern Iraqi Kurdistan, into which thousands Syrian Kurd's today seek asylum, is safe, secure and growingly prosperous.

The Kurds fell into a decade long civil war after the first Iraq invasion of the 1990s. Kurdish peace was established in the early 2000's and autonomy was recognised in the Iraqi Constitution. Today the Kurds have their own parliament, their own president, their own armed forces and their own passport control that issues their own visas.

On a spring day the central square of Iraqi Kurdistan's capital Erbil is a bustling place of small coffee shops, hookah-pipes bubbling the sweet scent of apple, families, children and fountains. Friendly and engaging locals seek to engage foreigners in a part Arabic, part English, part Kurdish discussion on geopolitics, the state of the region and the present day Iraq.

The Kurds will tell you that they may not be fans of George W Bush, but they will remind you of the brutal repression by Hussein. Discussions are held in the certain knowledge that without the western intervention Kurds would have neither freedom nor security to discuss anything with anyone.

There are winners as well as losers from the Iraq conflict. The winners were not just oil companies. Many of the winners are normal, innocent people like you and me, in this case the Kurds. But the flip side to the current Kurdish freedom is the huge expense to people elsewhere in the country.

The dilemma, balance and 'grey' is the real lesson of Iraq when thinking about Syria.

War has costs and benefits that can be measured in human lives and livelihoods that planners must balance. In discussions planners and observers must weigh up perceived costs and benefits of both action and inaction, even if both alternatives seem unpalatable. At the end of the day a choice between competing bad options must be made.

While Iraqi Kurdistan shows us the benefit to some of the last war, Iraq also shows us cost. The anti-war group 'Iraqi Body

Count' have worked to get as accurate data as possible and claim in the range of 112,000-123,000 needless deaths in the decade long war and aftermath.

Who's side to we take in looking at the intervention in Iraq, the Kurdish beneficiaries, or those that paid the price?

If it is decided decide that war costs too much, can we walk away with clean hands? What about the cost of 'no war'? Does Iraq provide guidance there?

In the decade before the war Hussein was estimated by Human Rights Watch and Amnesty International to have killed somewhere between 500,000 and 1 million people. What would Saddam have done if he stayed in power? Could we assume a personality change? Could we assume a peaceful transition to a democratic government?

Perhaps it would it be safer to assume a continuation of that which went before: mass murder on an industrial scale. Could the cost of 'no intervention' have been an additional 500,000 Iraqis killed by Hussein? We will never know for sure but absent a major change in the Hussein regime, reasonable hypothecation points to one heck of a moral dilemma if non-intervention kills more innocent people than intervention.

The world has experienced this before. The world saw hundreds of thousands of needless death in Bosnia through non-intervention. The world saw up to a million dead through non-intervention in Rwanda, even when the genocide plans were known to the Security Council in advance.

The same dilemma now exists with Syria. Would there be a huge toll if we were to have another international intervention? Undoubtedly yes. Intervention would be a bad option.

But what of non-intervention? President Assad is already the second of his line to rule that country having been anointed by his father. For how much longer would he and his offspring rule?

As with Iraq in 2002 there is no way of either accurately predicting the toll of an intervention or the toll of a non-intervention and choices need to be made on best guesses. This generation clearly remembers Iraq and the cost of the intervention. This generation's memory of Rwanda and Bosnia has faded as the cost of non-intervention drifts into history books.

The only thing we know for sure is that the moral dilemma continues. Are we happy for Syria to be our new Bosnia for fear of it being another Iraq?

East Timor: The Good Guys Won This One.

Introduction

In 1975 the father of my primary school friend was killed in East Timor. In 1999 I was able to play a small role in observing the independence Referendum, followed by training of pro-democracy activists in 2000 and finally to attend the hand-over to full Timorese sovereignty in 2002. It took a long time, but finally the good guys won. This is my perspective.

Rwanda is a funny place to start a discussion about East Timor – but it is relevant.

The 1994 Rwandan Genocide, the only genuine Genocide since WWII, left nearly 1 million people dead in 100 days. The post WWII calls of 'never again' sounded especially hollow against the revelations that the UN had advance notice of the Rwandan killing. UN member states could have prevented the 1 million deaths, but chose not to.

The 'good men' stayed silent and many people died.

I worked in Rwanda and images of that country remain with me.

In 1999 I found myself in East Timor as an observer at the independence referendum. This was, in part, a personal journey for me. My best friend in primary school was the son of one of the Australian journalists killed in 1975 and our families remain friends still.

As an eight going on nine year old, the death of Greg Shackleton in 1975 was an early lesson for me in the world of International Politics – a world that often abandoned people in a search for statistics and political stability. No matter how hard this lesson was for me, it was harder for my friend who has lived life without a father.

Along with many others, I hoped for years for a free expression of will for the people of East Timor. A seemingly forlorn desire became an unexpected reality as the Asian financial crisis and considerable political change pushed Indonesia into accepting a UN sponsored referendum.

There was, at last, hope that a wrong could be righted. Perhaps, I thought, international politics could spit out the right answer.

Following the announcement of the referendum result the killing that filled Australia's consciousness started. Instead of stepping in and stopping the killing the 'International Community' was pulling out, seemingly abandoning the people of East Timor to their fate. Images of Rwanda came back to my mind.

Would the world stand by and watch death re-visit us on a monumental scale? Would the world stand by and do nothing?

Fortunately intervention came, partly through leadership of the Australian people, and the Australian Government behind them. The killing stopped and a process of transferring East Timor to the people of East Timor began.

Last Sunday I was lucky enough to attend the Independence Day ceremony and to witness the culmination of the 25 year struggle for freedom and justice. The UN flag would come down and be replaced by the new standard of East Timor. Sovereignty would peacefully transfer and the referendum result would become effective. I would witness the first ever birth of a nation that passed through a UN transitional administration. Justice would be done and Greg's death would in part mean something. Closure could begin.

The ceremony had many highlights. The children danced for the future of Timor. Former Falantil guerrillas symbolically passed the new East Timor Flag to the new East Timor Defence Force.

The guerrillas carried no weapons and wore t-shirts, not fatigues. The symbol was strong. The guerrilla movement was dead, not because they were beaten, but because they won.

A group once branded 'terrorists' were handing over their struggle to a new government. The new government will now face the challenge of building their country – it is a challenge perhaps larger than gaining independence.

As powerful as the ceremony of handover was, it was not the closing of a chapter for me – that came a day later.

Greg Shackleton's widow, Shirley, and I went to visit a 'free' Balibo, the town in which Greg and four other journalists were killed in 1975.

A day after Timor achieved its independence we visited the house in which her husband was killed and the house upon which the journalists painted our national flag in the vein hope of protection from the invading Indonesian Army.

The image of the journalists painting the flag is one that helped galvanise Australian Public opinion to Timor's cause, even when our governments failed to lead us.

Shirley and I quietly chatted about events. We rang her son and spoke of the celebrations and the ceremony marking the independence.

Although many issues surrounding the deaths of the Balibo Five remain, a door has begun to close. We still need to know what the Australian government knew. We still need to know exactly what happened to Greg and his colleagues. It would be good to know where their remains are.

Challenges remain for the Timorese also. They need our help to build a country; particularly over the next few months as the UN pull out starves their economy.

But a process has ended and some personal closure has been achieved. Many people died but a good result has come. – This time, the good guys won.

C: NATURAL DISASTERS

Pakistan, finally, some good news.

Introduction

On October 85hth, 2005 and Massive earthquake struck northern Pakistan. The 'quake killed 73,338 people, including 20,000 schoolchildren. While the "headline" death figure may have been lower than the tsunami but all other figures were much larger. Over 128,000 people were injured. Three and a half million people were displaced. Over 600,000 houses, 6,400 km (3,977 miles) of road network, 6,298 education facilities, 350 health facilities, 3,994 water supply systems and 949 government buildings were all destroyed in approximately one minute.

Whilst the death toll was lower than the tsunami-affected countries, the level of destruction was twice that of all the tsunami countries combined.

I was sent to Pakistan in 2005 as part of the team dispatched to coordinate the massive Earthquake relief. I wrote this after about four month's relief effort.

Multimedia (ebook only)

You can see sample interviews I did on the earthquake relief at the time here and here. You can also see a video on how the earthquake relief was managed, here. This last video gives a sense of the size, scale and the magnificent terrain of Pakistan.

The valleys are deep in Kashmir, and the mountains tall. It is a breath-taking landscape that, if it were not an internationally recognized cease-fire line between two nuclear powers technically a war, it would be a tourist playground.

February 8th will mark, around the Line of Control, four months since the massive earthquake that struck the northern parts of Pakistan and Kashmir, both Indian and Pakistani controlled – and the story of the relief effort is a good one.

Let us first look at the situation four months ago: The earthquake struck minutes after the start of school hours. Within two minutes, most schools were destroyed killing approximately 35,000 children. A similar number of adults were killed. 73,000 deaths, 140,000 injuries, 3.5 million made homeless. All of the health infrastructure destroyed, and a cold, brutal Himalayan winter but weeks away.

This earthquake covered 30,000 square kilometres, an area larger than the areas affected by the tsunami. The logistics challenges were larger than those of the tsunami, mainly caused by the mountainous terrain. Tragically, the weather imposed a time deadline that did not have an equal in the tropical regions affect by the tsunami.

Fast forward now to February. Seven hundred thousand tents have been distributed, 300,000 emergency shelters built, 350,000 children immunized against measles – the simple disease that is the biggest killer in post disaster situations. There are 2,400 Cuban doctors, some working out of tents provided by the United States, more than 60 mobile hospitals, 20 mobile childbirth units, and 3.5 million receiving food aid.

By all medical criteria, the population in the affected region are in better shape today, than this time last year - a remarkable achievement.

What have been factors that have led to this success? There are three: One has been the remarkable weather. Whilst it is still cold above 5,000 feet, so far the Himalayan foothills have escaped remarkably lightly with a mild winter. If there is a higher power, may He be merciful and allow this to continue.

Secondly, the International Humanitarian Community has experimented with a new 'Cluster Approach' to natural disaster response that has so far led to an improved delivery, with two things missing - massive duplication, and huge un-met gaps.

Thirdly, and most importantly, has been an unanticipated openness and cooperation from the Pakistan Military in their most sensitive regions. Prior to the earthquake only a handful of foreigners were allowed in Kashmir. Now there are many hundreds.

There is a joint air tasking cell, where the UN, the US and Pakistan Military jointly task all air assets as one. Each of the three coordinating Pakistani generals in the field works with the UN and humanitarian system in jointly deciding priorities on food, health, water and sanitation and other emergency response systems.

At the national level, the military led Federal Relief Commission has at its heart a Strategic Planning cell made up of the Pakistan Army, the UN and major donors where information is analysed, and decisions taken – jointly.

Now whilst one may be tempted to say that 'this is nothing special, it is how it should work', the truth is that it has never happened this well before. Aid workers are now saying this is the best example of civil and military cooperation – anywhere, ever.

And in this sensitive region, on the front line of the so called 'war on terror', Islam and Christianity have worked together. Christian aid workers sat for Eid, celebrating the end of Ramadan. The 25th of December saw the entire affected region littered with signs wishing 'our Christian brothers and sisters a joyous day'. Christmas gifts were given and friendships strengthened. Radicals may exist, but so far they have remained focused on the relief effort.

In this disaster humanity has come together reminding us that despite those radicals that may wish to bomb buildings, or retaliation taken for those actions, despite cartoons of Mohammed or the protests against them, people are still people. Mothers still cry for lost children, fathers still blister hands shifting rubble and the young and the idealistic, from Turkey, United States, Cuba, Australia and other countries, descend to offer help, hope and expertise.

Despite the good news, more needs to be done. The winter may still hide tragedy. And its end will bring with it the challenge of decreased water quality due to snow melt, and incubation of disease due to increasing temperatures. The relief phase has not yet finished, and the re-building needs to begin – all of this needs on-going financial support.

The effort is far from over, yet Australian's can know that the Pakistani people are hardy, strong, and above all - just like us. They struggle against a huge natural disaster, and all they want is for their family to be safe, they want their schools open again, and they want to re-build their lives. The struggle is hard enough. Don't make them struggle against misconceptions, prejudice, religious intolerance, or financial devastation.

Non-Interfering Coordination, the Lessons behind the Pakistan Earthquake Relief.

Introduction

This article was co-written by the Vice Chief of General Staff of the Pakistan Army Lt Gen Nadeem Ahmed and me.

Multimedia (ebook only)

This was first published in the Center for Excellence in Disaster Management publication, The Liaison <u>here</u>, in 2008.

You can also see a video on how the earthquake relief was managed, <u>here</u>. Also there is a video on the 'fun' parts of Pakistan *<u>here</u>* and my reflections on leaving Pakistan *<u>here</u>*.

In October 2005 Northern Pakistan suffered a massive earthquake that left a humanitarian need twice that of all the tsunami-affected countries combined. Added to this, a brutal Himalayan winter was only six weeks away. Yet there was no massive second wave of deaths, and the method of civil-military cooperation in ensuring disaster response has been labelled as a model. How did this work?

Lt. Gen. Nadeem Ahmed, then Vice Chief of Pakistan's General Staff, and Andrew MacLeod, then Chief of Operations for the UN Emergency Coordination Centre and Cluster Coordinator, examine key lessons from what is now regarded as both a successful relief operation, and a template for civil and military cooperation.

Whilst some may have heard of the earthquake, few realise just how large it was in terms of emergency relief – yet it was both huge and hugely successful. We will analyse the Pakistan disaster response success in five steps. We will review the size of the calamity, why the military was and should be used, review why Non-Governmental Organizations (NGOs) and international assistance was needed, explain the model of "non-interfering coordination," and look at how the new "Cluster System" assisted in humanitarian delivery. Finally, we will list key lessons learned to be adapted for future emergencies.

The Size

The earthquake killed 73,338 people, including 20,000 schoolchildren. While the "headline" death figure may have been lower than the tsunami, all other figures were much larger. Over 128,000 people were injured. Three and a half million people were displaced. Over 600,000 houses, 6,400 km (3,977 miles) of road network, 6,298 education facilities, 350 health facilities, 3,994 water supply systems and 949 government buildings were all destroyed in approximately one minute.

Whilst the death toll was lower than the tsunami-affected countries, the level of destruction was twice that of all the tsunami countries combined. For example, the tsunami destroyed less than 200,000 houses and displaced about one and a half million people. In addition, Pakistan's climate required a massive and rapid response just 6 weeks before a brutal Himalayan winter was due to strike in a mere six weeks. This winter would cut links to thousands of people, and deep snow would close remaining roads and render the earthquake survivors incredibly vulnerable.

Further disaster was predicted, and calamity seemed certain.

In response, the Pakistan Military launched a massive response. US, British, NATO and even Australian military forces all worked together under the Pakistan Government's leadership to provide relief to the ravaged region - as did thousands of NGO and United Nations (UN) staff members.

Why Use the Military At All?

But if there are thousands of international NGOs descending, let alone thousands of volunteer Pakistanis, why use the military at all? What is the military "value addition" to a humanitarian situation?

An emergency of this size cannot be dealt with by existing infrastructure and systems alone. With so many government structures and key personnel wiped out, a rapid replacement of capacity is needed. Also, many people will arrive offering assistance and looking for an effective interlocutor. Someone has to be that focal point.

So why the military?

The military has assets, mobility, means, organisation and wherewithal, and can provide national, district and local coordination infrastructure for NGOs, civil society and international support to "plug in to." Most importantly, they can work in distant areas, hard-to-reach and perhaps "insecure" regions. The military, particularly if well trained, has knowledge and the ability to think and adapt.

But then again, if the military is so good, why use NGOs or other actors at all?

Whilst the military may have some knowledge on fighting wars, peacekeeping operations and control in civil strife, they often do not have in a traditional set-up any knowledge or expertise specific to humanitarian operations. Nor do they usually have the understanding of the political paradigm that exists in the middle of a humanitarian operation.

The military specifically lacks advance practice and training in critical standards, such as the SPHERE standards, that give guidelines on almost everything in humanitarian assistance.1 Do military forces know how to set up "child-friendly spaces" within a camp? They may know neat rows of tents, but do they know that by angling a tent more privacy is given to an individual family? Does a military force understand the importance of privacy?

Does a sub-unit commander know how to construct a female-sensitive latrine, and ensure its accessibility and proper lighting in order to reduce a female's vulnerability to sexual and gender-based violence? Does the army collect sex-disaggregated data and understand its importance in planning, monitoring and mid-course corrections?

Does the military know how to set up an internally displaced person (IDP) returns process and ensure that aid deliveries in a relief operation do not cause a long-term "dependency syndrome"?

Most military personnel globally would have received no training in any of the above concepts, let alone know how to implement them. Yet the military has an enormous capacity to provide logistical support. Nevertheless, without the help of humanitarian experts, it cannot use its logistical and manpower strengths. It must, therefore, be willing to learn and adapt.

Death, cold, starvation and thirst are enemies in humanitarian operations, not an opposing military force. Hence, when operating in the humanitarian environment, the military needs to change its mind-set.

Working with the International Humanitarian Community

There is an enormous challenge for a host government, and particularly a host military, when dealing with the international humanitarian community. However, knowledge and experience in humanitarian and natural disaster response exists within NGOs and other humanitarian agencies, both national and international. It must be tapped into so that the maximum benefit is gained from the military's logistical skill. Their respective skill sets and intrinsic capabilities must combine to produce optimal results.

Additionally, particularly in a large disaster, international organisations, such as the United Nations, can help to mobilise resources, give understanding of the political dimension and provide a coordination network referenced later in this article.

Whilst humanitarian organisations and the military may not be natural bed-fellows, they both must learn to adapt and coordinate with each other in disaster settings.

NGOs, in particular, are often grouped into one category, whereas in reality they are vastly different, ranging from "one-man" operations to multi-national professional organisations. However, there are some characteristics most NGOs have in common.

Firstly, NGOs guard their "independence" and "mandates." Some, such as Médicins Sans Frontières (MSF) and Care International, guard their principles and mandates in international charters. One may even see more than one part of the same organisation. One may see MSF Holland, MSF Belgium, and MSF France – perhaps working with each other and perhaps working independently. Some, like the Red Cross Movement, have their independence and mandates enshrined in international documents and treaties.

Secondly, and deriving from this, NGOs rarely, if ever, accept a "tasking order" from the military.

Thirdly, whilst a military commander may be trained to coordinate by control, the coordination of NGOs is more by persuasion and less by control; more by diplomacy and less by orders. So how does a military or civilian operational commander seek and gain visibility over an entire operation, if a key component of that operation has the skills and knowledge needed, but will not be controlled?

The authors suggest that the military can prepare for interacting with the international humanitarian community.

In all military operations the maxim "Prior Preparation and Planning Prevents Poor Performance" applies. Subsequently, if military forces are being used more often in disaster response, and as climate change experts predict more natural disasters, the military should train more for these types of operations.

We would suggest, that at a minimum, military units should be trained in the SPHERE standards and understand the basic coordination paradigm. Whilst the army coordinates by control – an order is given and an order is followed – the NGO world does not work like this. Coordination in the NGO world is by persuasion and consensus – not by control.

This is extremely frustrating for a military commander, but the situation merits the old saying: "Give me the strength to change the things I can, the serenity to leave the things I cannot, and the wisdom to know the difference." A military commander may try to change the paradigm, but he will not succeed, or at least not enough to positively affect the outcome of an operation. So a military commander must understand the paradigm, master it and thereby control the outcome, if not the process. In the case of the Pakistan Response, we termed this "non-interfering coordination".

Non-Interfering Coordination

Many aspects of the earthquake response were experimental. In seeking to bridge the military world and the NGO world, a new model was tried. This "non-interfering coordination" (a term first coined by the authors in a planning meeting at General Headquarters Rawalpindi, Pakistan's main military headquarters) was used to build the bridge.

The theory behind this concept is as follows:

- Share an open and honest assessment of needs with the NGO and humanitarian world, including the United Nations.
- Allow humanitarian actors to choose what operations they will undertake, rather than dictate activities.
- Ask NGOs to inform central commanders of the choices made.
- Central commanders can then identify unmet gaps in humanitarian delivery, which can then be back-filled with the Army and other government agencies.

This sounds simple, and in theory it is. However, in practice, consolidating that information, and tracking and monitoring the promised "delivery" is extremely difficult and challenging both for the military and for NGOs – both have to fight institutional reflexes that prevent them from sharing with each other. On the positive side, this mechanism means that independence of NGOs can be respected, whilst their activities can be coordinated with the backfilling efforts of the military forces.

Collating, consolidating and sharing information within the humanitarian community is difficult in itself, even when removed from a need to coordinate with the military. In August 2005 the humanitarian community went through a process called "Humanitarian Response Review" to streamline their own coordination, which was launched by the UN Office for the Coordination of Humanitarian Affairs (UN OCHA). The humanitarian world understands many of its deficiencies in response and is endeavouring to improve. The "Humanitarian Response Review" process created a series of recommendations by UN and non-UN entities for reform called "The Cluster Approach" and seeks to improve the effectiveness of humanitarian response by ensuring greater predictability, accountability and partnership.

In essence, this "Cluster Approach" divides up humanitarian response into a number of sectors including, but not limited to: health, food, water and sanitation, camp management, shelter etc. An agency takes responsibility for that sector (eg. World Health Organization [WHO] for health, the Red Cross for some shelter scenarios, the World Food Program [WFP] for food), and aims to coordinate and have visibility over that sector.

Through the Cluster System, the humanitarian actors can be asked to ensure that there is no duplication of action, and no unknown and unmet gaps – or at least try to.

In Pakistan the military adapted to the Cluster System. Indeed, for the military "clustered" thinking is the norm. The military already had a logistics corps, a medical corps, and the like, so they intellectually understood clustered coordination. By partnering military "clusters" with the humanitarian "clusters", a mechanism for identifying and filling gaps was created. In essence, the Clusters became the backbone of "non-interfering coordination" by being the hubs though which information was shared.

Clusters — Help or Hindrance?

As Pakistan had no designated National Disaster Agency at the time of the Earthquake, the ad-hoc structure created to deal with the aftermath (the Federal Relief Commission) decided to structure itself using the Cluster Approach as well.

What resulted was a rare, if not unique, series of key personal contacts between the national and international coordinators, and between civil and military actors within the Clusters. It was these personal contacts within the Cluster framework that allowed for the ironing out of some "perspective problems."

The Pakistan military often had the perspective of "what has been done." That is, it focused on "what has been done rather than what is left to be done." Military reports spoke of 35,000 tents delivered, or 15 tonnes of medical supplies delivered. The humanitarian world, on the other hand, brought with it a perspective of "what is left to be done" and would note that while "x" number of tents had been delivered, "y" number were still needed.

Whilst the difference in perspectives could cause problems, the ability to talk through issues and raise concerns within the context of Cluster meetings allowed for solutions to be found, rather than problems festering.

Ironically, the military found it easier to adapt to the new Cluster mechanism than did the humanitarian world.

Once senior military commanders understood the logic of Cluster Coordination and passed command orders down the chain, mid-level officers simply accepted the mechanism, as that is what they were ordered to do.

Within the world of humanitarian organisations, things were more difficult. When the Cluster System was tried for the first time in Pakistan, no pre-existing Terms of References (ToRs), guidance notes or pool of experience existed. Additionally, when the Cluster System was rolled out earlier than planned because of the unexpected timing of the quake, many NGOs had not received "guidance" let alone "orders" to implement the system.

The Clusters thereby became not only the method of internal humanitarian coordination, but by virtue of a military presence in the Cluster meetings, the system also became the heart of the civil-military coordination structure.

Whilst there were problems in the implementation of the Cluster Approach, the system allowed for them to be overcome cooperatively. It is a system designed to improve humanitarian coordination amongst humanitarian actors, and proved its worth in the Pakistan Earthquake Response by creating a structure for overall engagement between national and international actors, humanitarians and the military.

One excellent example of the system was the "Air Operations Cell" created in Pakistan. All aircraft – Pakistan, US, UK military and United Nations owned and operated – were tasked out of a common tasking cell. Cargo was designated to aircraft by cargo and location requirements, not by ownership of cargo and aircraft. This meant some 100 plus available airframes were optimally used even though individual "ownership and control" were diluted.

One further example was successfully dealing with cross-cutting issues, such as human rights and gender, and environmental factors, as well as issues that affect more than one Cluster, such as import restrictions. At its peak, Humanitarian Cluster Leaders (mainly UN) met with Government Cluster leaders (mainly military) in the Strategic Leaders Group (SLG). This group engaged all sectors and was the ultimate governing body of the Pakistan Response. Whilst strong national leadership was maintained, joint decision making with national, international, civil and military partners was also achieved.

Despite difficulties in implementing a new system in the midst of a major emergency, the Cluster Approach in Pakistan produced the facts, which speak for themselves:

- One million tents, 6 million blankets, 400,000 emergency shelters delivered or built through a coordinated and consolidated effort. Military and humanitarian logistics capacities were combined and cargo allocated according to need, not dispatching agency.
- 350,000 internally displaced persons (IDPs) housed over winter, with 95% returning in the first year after the relief – through a unique combination of humanitarian and military management.
- No second wave of deaths in the ensuing winter, and in fact, all medical measures showed an improved rate of cold-related infections over normal years.
- All schools and hospitals functional; first in emergency setting, and in transitional setting.
- Largest single relief effort ever.

Statistics like those listed above, and a recognition of the joint role of the military and the NGOs in the clusters led to Jan Vandemoortele, the United Nations Humanitarian Coordinator in Pakistan, to dubbing the operation "[The] most successful civil and military cooperation ever."

Whilst the system may not be the one a military force is used to, it is the one international humanitarian players will use in the future. A military commander may be tempted to use his own command and control system instead of the Cluster's cooperative approach, but to try and control or change the international system too much, or not done in full consultation, with transparency and within the spirit of humanitarian delivery, the commander will be doing the operation a great disservice by creating nothing but confusion, turmoil and mistrust.

Conversely, NGOs may seek to fight a new system, or maintain a reluctance to share information, but doing so will also reduce service delivery to the people in need.

In summary, the unusual but key non-interfering coordination process utilized the Cluster approach by the following process: once gaps had been identified, the approach of military commanders was to allow NGOs to freely choose which of the gaps they could fill and then having NGOs report progress back to a Cluster meeting. Residual gaps were then back-filled by the military and also reported back to Cluster meetings.

In the end, the Clusters provided a mechanism for information and idea exchange between civil and military actors alike, enabling the non-interfering coordination process to occur. A sharing of a common understanding of who is doing what and where allowed for gaps to be identified. The level of information-sharing seen in the Pakistan earthquake was, in the opinion of the authors, rare if not unique among disaster response situations.

Lessons Learned

The authors provide the following suggestions as lessons learned for national authorities, including the military, from the Pakistan earthquake:

- Analyse and modify the United Nations "Cluster Coordination" concept in consultation with the actors on the ground and the needs of the operation.
- Start big, and scale back, not start small and grow.
- Absorb knowledge and be willing to experiment.
- Joint Logistics is better than individual control.
- A Strategic Leaders Group helps integrated planning and response. It is a sign of strength in national confidence to seek out support while maintaining leadership.
- Particularly for the military we see the following as critical:
- A willingness to open up, share information and admit areas of weakness produces better results.
- Willing to learn and set priorities based on new, non-military dynamics.
- Willing to reach consensus, not insist on command.
- Backfill gaps through non-interfering coordination.
- Experiment and be bold in employment.
- Develop capacities and train in advance (for example SPHERE Standards)

- Regionally engage in exercises and response – including with the UN's International Search and Rescue Advisory Group (INSARAG), the United Nations Disaster Assessment and Coordination (UNDAC) team and other mechanisms.
- Have sufficient resources in stock for immediate response, nationally and regionally.
- Share and absorb knowledge and best practices.
- Must assist the assimilation of foreign militaries that come to assist.

Many of these recommendations can be achieved with a structured, yet short, training program to include:

- SPHERE standards training.
- The Humanitarian Paradigm: Training in NGO cultures and methodologies.
- Training and an understanding of humanitarian coordination systems such as the Cluster Approach.

If these issues are trained and rehearsed in advance in standard Command Post exercises, and together with NGOs and UN agencies, we believe that the above lessons can contribute to a more successful operation. Like in all other areas of military operation, one must rehearse, rehearse and rehearse.

For NGOs, a similar training program to gain an understanding of SPHERE, humanitarian coordination, the military culture and how militaries work, would be of equal benefit.

Above all, any military force must accept that until they are trained in humanitarian operations, they are not the experts at humanitarian response. The humanitarians are. When responding to crisis situations, the military should use and adapt humanitarian knowledge and experience, and not be afraid of it. On the other hand, humanitarians must understand that the military has an enormous logistical capacity that can also be used. By working together, each can improve their results.

Victorian Bushfires: With proper planning we'll bounce back

Introduction

Following the tragic bushfires in Victoria I wrote to the Victorian Government with advice based on international experience. Their response: That only applies in third world countries. Unfortunately that is not correct. Lessons can be applied across the board in natural disaster response. It is interesting to compare the circumstances in the fire affected regions now.

Multimedia (ebook only)

The following article was first published in The Age here on February 11, 2009.

I have also spoken on impacts of planning and aid here.

INTERNATIONAL experience tells us that the sooner the planning for reconstruction begins, the better it is both for the communities affected and for the ultimate results. The United Nations even suggests that post-disaster reconstruction planning take place before a disaster - that is, when contingency planning is made.

So what now for Victoria? Federal and state politicians, together with community leaders, have a critical role. In the United Nations experience, successful post-disaster recovery depends on how fast critical decision-makers can change their focus from the immediate disaster to the rehabilitation, how these decision-makers can mobilise communities to look forward.

The appointment of Christine Nixon therefore is a good move. We in the United Nations often advise governments to immediately pull someone out of the immediate emergency response and have them look to reconstruction. Hence the Victorian Government so far has acted smartly.

In our post-disaster recovery work we often use the catchphrase "Build Back Better". It is catchphrase that Victorians could use now.

It is critical to accept the disaster, to grieve and to mourn lost friends, but then focus on creating the desire to rebuild and to seize the opportunity to improve on what came before.

For example, the destruction of Marysville, the beautiful town I have spent many pleasant afternoons in, is devastating. But, in rebuilding it, what can we do to improve it? We have an opportunity to work with the community to look at road layout, critical infrastructure, rezoning and see if the balance in the new Marysville can improve on the old.

There is always a temptation to rebuild communities the way they were - the same schools, facilities and so on. However, total destruction, while tragic, gives a great opportunity to review the community's infrastructure and ask whether changes should be made.

The same will apply to Kinglake and Kinglake West. I often had a dim sim in the Beales' store before heading down the road to St Andrews. I mourn the loss of friends there, but can we rebuild Kinglake and Kinglake West back even better? What would the communities like to see improved or changed?

Building Back Better, therefore, may not be building back the same. Now is the time to work with the communities to help reconstruct their lives and their towns, and the sooner it starts the better.

The sooner political and community leaders can get together and start working - by first analysing what was there before and then deciding what should be built back - the better.

There may be a temptation to keep focus on the immediate disaster, but I would urge decision-makers to get together with state MPs and councillors and form community reconstruction groups, to support Christine Nixon in her work and to improve the communities.

As well as resulting in better planning, the psycho-social aspects of getting a community to look forward, in my experience, results in better and stronger communities.

For this reason school classes must begin as soon as they can - in temporary, portable or relocated classrooms. Returning children to school has two great impacts. First, it allows children to begin to get a sense of normality. The psycho-social impact of this is positive. But second, it also frees parents from the day-to-day child-care burden, allowing them to concentrate on critical issues for their family's future. Will they rebuild? Where? What will their livelihood be?

And on the subject of livelihoods, we need great thought and great care in building back our communities. The rural livelihoods need support for restocking and reseeding. The tourism industry, however, will be much tougher.

Again for Marysville, and the other many small and beautiful towns throughout the fire-affected region, the attraction of large trees, dense forests and beautiful nature are many years from fully re-establishing themselves.

So while Nixon has a challenge to meet the infrastructure needs, the livelihood needs will also prove a great challenge.

While we commend and support the on-going work of the emergency response volunteers, the CFA, the Red Cross and many other volunteers, we need to support also the long and difficult task that Nixon and her colleagues will have over the coming years, to restore and rebuild livelihoods and lifestyles of the people so tragically struck down.

D: AID, AID WORKERS NEW WAYS TO DO AID

Why aid workers are now in the crosshairs

Introduction

Aid workers are courageous people. During my time in the UN and Red Cross friend of mine died in the line of their duty. We sometimes forget how dangerous aid work can be. However the plaintive cry of 'neutrality' as a protecting force is losing its power. Why is that? In this article I put the view that because humanitarian agencies indirectly assist the US, they are a target.

Multimedia (ebook only)

This article was first published in The Age here on 26 November 2003.

On August 19 a bomb exploded outside the UN compound in Iraq killing 24 humanitarian workers and injuring another 150. On October 27 at least 12 were killed at the International Committee of the Red Cross office in Baghdad. On November 17, 29-year-old Bettina Goislard was murdered while on duty with the UN High Commissioner for Refugees in Afghanistan.

Why were these organisations targeted? The answer is frightening for humanitarian workers: they are targets because they are providing humanitarian aid.

In simple military terms, one attacks an enemy where the enemy is most vulnerable.

The objective of the United States, and its coalition of occupying powers, is to restore stability in Iraq. Indeed, the Fourth Geneva Convention requires the occupying power to maintain peace and security and provide all items indispensable for the survival of the civilian population.

Feeding a population is hard work and the US military is not set up to do it; rather, the military is structured to defeat an enemy military force. This is recognised by planners who, in the US and most major military organisations these days, have established dedicated CiMiC (or Civilian-Military Co-operation) units to co-ordinate the humanitarian delivery to vulnerable populations.

CiMiC structures help fulfil the military's obligations and by helping co-ordinate the delivery of vital supplies, aid the return of stability to a country. In other words, the humanitarian organisations coincidentally help the military achieve the military's overall objective.

Viewed through the eyes of the anti-US forces in Iraq, coalition vulnerability is represented by humanitarian workers.

Contrary to the US aims, the objective of either the Iraq bombers or the murderers of Bettina Goislard is to disrupt the supply of assistance to the civilian population and maintain disorder in their country.

More disorder and disruption to aid supplies increases disquiet within the civilian populations. And, if the aid agencies continue to scale back or pull out, it puts the pressure back on the US-led military forces to deliver the aid needed by the population.

Aid delivery stretches scarce military resources and requires the force to move bulky cargo in strategically vulnerable convoys open to easy attack.

Anti-coalition forces may thus think that attacks on the UN and the Red Cross disrupt aid supply, increase disquiet in the community, enhance the opportunity for recruitment to their cause, and increase the number of vulnerable soft military targets on the road.

Not a bad result, from their perspective.

A more frightening way of looking at this is to say the more efficient and effective a humanitarian organisation is, the more important a target it is in the eyes of the anti-US forces.

The effective delivery of humanitarian supplies is what makes the UN a target, precisely because the delivery undermines one side of the conflict and helps the other.

So what do we do?

Big agencies rightly refuse to pay ransom when a staff member is kidnapped. The reason is simple - if you pay ransom you encourage more kidnapping. Now the stakes are higher. If aid organisations pull out when international staff are killed, doesn't this just encourage the targeting of the undefended humanitarian workers? But if staff members are not pulled out in places such as Iraq and perhaps now Afghanistan, their mere work makes them a target for attacks.

Running concurrently with this is the huge growth in "privatised military corporations", or PMCs, that are subcontracted to provide security and training and, in some cases, deliver aid.

So what should the international community do? Do we hand responsibility for delivery of humanitarian aid to military structures? Do we subcontract aid delivery to the PMCs or, in the hope of maintaining some neutrality, do we ask humanitarian workers to do their work knowing that they are unarmed and undefended targets?

In the old days of African hunting, men pegged innocent goats to the ground knowing they would attract prey and could not defend themselves. Will humanitarian workers become the new "pegged goats"?

Have Australian companies maximised their advantage?

If good business is to engage development and environmental concerns in a productive manner, then there exists an enormous potential for positive action beyond what has so far been explored. The most successful companies are looking to align these win-win opportunities with their business models.

Why Go it Alone in Community Development?

Introduction

During my decade and a half in the aid world, I became more disillusioned with the lack of effectiveness in the delivery of aid. A lot of money was spent, but few results. Corporates, on the other hand, have started to see it in their interest to have sustainable economic growth. Could we have a new model?

Multimedia (ebook only)

This was first published at the Harvard Business Review on June 13, 2002, here.

Drive down a typical highway and you'll see a succession of billboards, each one a stand-alone advertisement for a single brand. Watch a Grand Prix race, on the other hand, and you note a different approach: every car carries a multitude of brands. These complicated, high-performance machines are expensive to build and maintain. With just one sponsor, a car wouldn't amount to much.

Now think about how companies approach their community development and CSR programs. Much like billboards, today's community-oriented efforts are undertaken independently, and proudly associated with single company names. What if companies thought of community programs more like Grand Prix cars? What if they recognized the vast support communities often need, and partnered up to provide it? Presumably it would serve the communities better if CSR programs adopted the Grand Prix rather than the billboard model. Probably it would also be more profitable for the firms.

My company is in the resource extraction business, and it has known for a long time how these two things, communities and corporate interests, can go hand in hand. My company understands that we do not operate in a bubble.

In some parts of the world government mismanagement of community development (deliberate or otherwise) has led to civil strife, sometimes resulting in armed conflict, creating a security scenario where business simply cannot continue to operate. Even when peace has returned, post-conflict nationalization has been seen in many countries, with business losing billions in operational assets. Looking at history, business cannot afford to be not interested in community development. A company simply has too much to lose if things go wrong.

Increasingly, we've seen other companies recognize equitable community development as a critical business activity to reduce risk. This is a major change. In decades past, it would not have been uncommon for business leaders to say that it is a government's responsibility to ensure long-term sustainable economic growth for a community, and that a company's contribution would be through tax, employment, and royalties. Move forward to 2012, and those days are long gone. Most now recognize that business can't legitimately claim that socio-economic development is not a business concern.

At this point, some companies are looking beyond the risk-reduction argument, and seeing in equitable community development an opportunity to grow "shared value." The term was coined by Michael Porter and Mark Kramer, and reflects the view that business and community interests can be in sync. In particular, Porter and Kramer argue that businesses should search for those opportunities where value can be created for business by improving community well-being.

BHP Billiton for example ran a very effective anti-malaria program around Mozal, Mozambique where it has an aluminium smelter. This program reduced adult malaria infection from near 80% to a single-digit percentage. This is a huge win for the community, but also note its impact on BHP's bottom line. The reduced absenteeism associated with this improved community health so increased the productivity of assets that the direct returns more than covered the cost of the program. The anti-malaria program in Mozal was *profitable*.

The Australian based bank ANZ offers another example as it expands throughout the Asia Pacific. Its community development work in places like Fiji, American Samoa, and the Cook Islands focuses on financial literacy training programs. Cynics might well say that in educating people about the workings of small business loans or mortgages it is just expanding its market. On the other hand, who could deny that better informed people are more able to benefit from services we take for granted in the developed world? What is wrong with prospering along with a community empowered by greater skills in budgeting, saving, and money management?

Neither of these cases should be viewed as corporate philanthropy; both are investments with returns to community and the business's owners being measured and celebrated. The contribution that Porter and Kramer make with their "shared value" concept is that it legitimizes such investments—community work motivated by considerations of what is good for business, and not just the work motivated by philanthropic altruism.

Rio Tinto is now the majority shareholder in the Development of the Oyu Tolgoi mine in Mongolia. When fully operational, this mine promises to account for somewhere between a quarter and a third of the GDP of Mongolia. Rio Tinto does not think that economic, community, and social development is none of its business. The successful expansion of Rio Tinto Copper is intertwined with the economic development of Mongolia and its people.

Back to the Grand Prix analogy. With so many companies now focused on community development, could we see more in the way of partnership? In other realms of economic activity, we see collaboration between non-competitor businesses as a path to improved shared profitability. Is there any reason we should not see it in community work?

Let's say a company is developing a new mine in a community that has seen little development. The resource company recognizes that the huge boost to economic activity will raise many challenges. Towns need to be built, and the influx of workers needs to be managed. As money moves into an economy that had little reliable money supplies, let alone banks, people need to be equipped to handle it. Should a resource company try to engage with all these problems relying on just itself and the government? It might think to partner with NGOs or UN agencies. But what about other companies?

The Grand Prix model might suggest to the resource company that it could contact a community-minded bank like ANZ, point to the potential of the community, and encourage it to invest there,

89

too. The community would then benefit from the first company employing and paying staff, and the second one accepting deposits, providing training, and extending credit as appropriate to those who could use it to build wealth. Why not then encourage a third company, a health company, to serve the growing healthcare needs of the community in a shared value mode—that is, setting goals and measuring outcomes for the community as well as setting itself up to operate profitably?

If companies join forces to build communities, rather than trying to go it alone, communities are better served. When benefits are wholly dependent on one party's continuing commitment, they are at the mercy of any catastrophic event that damages that party. Billboards can topple in a storm. With more partners comes more stability. Communities grow healthier and more productive, and progress comes on many fronts. The companies on board benefit, too, from the faster progress that comes with shared commitment—perhaps not as fast as a Grand Prix car, but at least as exhilarating.

Can doing the right thing improve corporate valuations?

Introduction

Community risk is the one area of risk that can destroy 100% of Net Present Value. So why do so many think Community Development Programs aimed at reducing risk are just 'green-washing'?

Some in the left wing find it hard to accept that there is a growing role of the private sector in playing a genuine and real role in community development. They are sceptical and think such programs are only 'green-washing'.

Equally some hard-nosed business leaders think such programs are done to protect the corporate reputation but provide little measurable benefit to the bottom line.

Both views can be wrong.

While many companies have 'Corporate Social Responsibility' (CSR) programs, leading companies have moved beyond CSR to 'Shared Value'. Leading companies do this not because they have taken a 'be nice' pill, but rather because leading companies now understand truly effective and non 'green-washing' community programs reduce community risk and thereby increase net present value (NPV) of their assets in non OECD economies.

In the resource sector for example, the value of a mine, ore body or natural resource is often expressed in terms of NPV. Put simply, NPV of the asset is calculated by subtracting Net Present Cost from the Net Present Revenue.

Net Present Revenue, in simple terms, is calculated by estimating future revenue over the life of an asset and subtracting from that figure a discount for things such as cost of holding money, sovereign risk and community risk.

Net Present Cost is calculated in a similar way for costs looking at the best estimates of asset construction and running costs over life of mine.

Genuinely reducing community risk can increase the value of assets as measured in today's balance sheets. Let me take you through a hypothetical and simplified example.

Let's say a mining company is looking to develop a new copper mine in a remote region with an estimated life of mine of 100 years. The Rio Tinto operated Oyu Tolgoi mine in Mongolia would be such a mine.

Let's hypothetically say the future costs of construction and operating the mine expressed in today's terms is $100 billion over the live of the mine.

Let's now say that estimated future revenue is $150 billion. Let's now discount that amount by 10% for the cost of holding money, 10% for community risk and 10% for sovereign risk factors. This would give a total discount on future revenue of $45 billion leaving Net Present Revenue of $105 billion. Taking from this the $100 billion in Net Present Cost leaves a NPV of $5 billion.

If the company were to implement a genuine community risk reduction process, and genuinely involve the community in discussions around issues of concern such that the community risk rating could be reduced from say 10% to 5%, lets see what happens to NPV.

NPR of $150b discounted by 10% for cost of holding money, 10% for sovereign risk and only 5% for community risk gives a 25% discount of $37.5b instead of $45b. NPV rises from $5b to $12.5b, more than doubling the value in today's balance sheet.

BHP Billiton and Rio Tinto, the two largest global mining companies, are well known for their risk reduction approach. They see this as a critical element of maintaining their positions among the lowest quartile cost producers in the commodities of their choice. A focus on cost reduction and risk reduction is the reason that commodity prices tend to stabilise above their cost of production ensuring long term profitability.

Let's examine another example.

Recently I was approached by a Chilean mining company and asked to advise on the transport of sulphuric acid from port to mine. The company had the choice between road and rail freight, with the rail option being slightly more expensive than road.

Management were leaning towards the road option because of the lower freight rate.

But how does risk factor into the overall value?

The lower freight rate of road will reduce the Net Present Cost of the operation and thereby increase NPV. But road transport has three significant risk factors that rail does not: Catastrophic spill, community dissatisfaction of road congestion and community dissatisfaction on particulate pollution.

The road option is likely to have a higher risk rating than rail, hence there should be a higher discount rate applied to future revenue and therefore reduce Net Present revenue. Hence the road option will both reduce net present cost and net present revenue.

The question is what happens to NPV? Does risk impact on value more than freight rate? Would rail, on balance be a better option? This is a question management often avoid answering because the calculation involves some degree of artistry rather than science. Good management must tackle this question though.

Here is another example. BHP Billiton, the world's largest mining company runs one of the world's most effective anti-malaria programs in Mozal Mozambique, not because it is nice, but because it increases value.

The company's program has reduced adult malaria infection from above 90% of the adult population to below 10%. The improved community health has lowered absenteeism in the work force and that has increased the productivity of their operation by a measurable amount higher than the cost of the program itself. When measured well, one can demonstrate that the anti-malaria program is directly, measurably profitable.

Additionally the company a lower the risk rating as the community genuinely values the mining company impact hence increasing NPV still further.

Here is a challenge of the investment industry: When valuing assets for prospective investment, are funds managers properly measuring community risk? If a company has a good community relationship that is not being analysed then the NPV will be underestimated and a good investment opportunity may be missed.

On the other hand, if a poor community relationship is not being measured then the NPV may be artificially inflated and you may be buying into a dud.

How much does this really matter? Well ask yourself this: Rio Tinto wrote of $3b in value from their Mozambique Coal assets recently. The asset was purchased for $4b, less than half a decade ago. That is ¾ of the value lost. How much of that write down was caused by the lack of gaining permits to use the Zambezi River as route to port for the coal? According to the company, a lot. And how much was community dissatisfaction involved in not gaining the permits?

Do Australian resource companies help local communities?

Introduction

This article poses the question: Is development aid really the way to go to bring the world out of poverty? Perhaps a well-focused company can do more good?

Multimedia (ebook only)

The following was first published in the Mining Journal published here on 22 July 2011.

Recently Australian resource companies have benefitted from improvements in health and education in the developing world and Australian indigenous populations. Smarter and healthier people have led to better, more productive workforces.

For example, in the late 1990's, adult malaria infections in Mozal, Mozambique stood at an astonishing 82%. Such a high rate of infection was debilitating for the community and made employment and investment difficult. An anti-malaria campaign was launched. Within three years, malaria infections were reduced to a mere 8% of the adult population. Employment and investment increased.

Recently an indigenous group in the Pilbara of Australia lacked clean drinking water causing their health to be so poor that they could not be employed. Fortunately a water supply was built making a community ready for work.

The communities clearly benefitted from these programs with improvement in quality of life indicators and by making the regions more ready for investment. At first glance, one would be forgiven for assuming that such programs must have been instigated by governments in conjunction with a United Nations or NGO initiatives.

However, these remarkably successful and widespread ventures were actually initiated by BHP Billiton and Atlas Iron.

Should these programs implemented from a business perspective, a community perspective, or a bit of both? How should programs like this be planned and success measured?

Companies realise that community Investment is often met with public scepticism created by the assumption that corporate gain should not be a motivating factor in community investment.

But why not? Why can't a program have both a community and a corporate benefit? How do we show that a link with profit is a positive and sustainable fact, rather than negative?

If developing economy employment can be aligned with long term corporate interests and positive returns to shareholders, doesn't this create the often sought after win-win scenario and a long term sustainable partnership?

Rio Tinto recently signed a land mark deal to guarantee long term investment in indigenous health, education and employment creation, in return for access to resources. Rio Tinto didn't just pay cash – an easy way out – they took a long term view to convert the area's natural resource into a human resource for the benefit the community, and yes, the shareholders.

According to the United Nations, $1 billion is spent per year through the core funding of the United Nations Development Program to attempt to alleviate global poverty.

Between BHP Billiton, ANZ, NAB and Rio Tinto nearly $500 million per year is spent on community investment programs. This is half of the UNDP core budget from just four companies with Community Investment heads based in Melbourne, Australia.

When you add in the rest of the world, it is estimated that corporate Community Investment is worth in excess of $59 billion per annum. The entire UN system, including peace-keeping and political affairs has a budget of around $15 billion. Corporate Community Investment exceeds the total amount of the entire UN budget by nearly four times.

Surely then we need to reassess our role as the private sector in development? We should look to synergies with private sector development *investment* not just public sector development *aid* that would improve both community benefit and return to shareholders?

In the 50 countries the Australian government has an aid program, nearly $5 billion is spent annually in aid, and nearly $90 billion is earned bilaterally in trade. Most of this trade is in resource rich countries where Australian resource companies are amongst the leading players.

Perhaps it is time to look at linking the aid and trade agendas for benefits to companies, communities and governments.

This leads us to the question, can we foster a culture that not only celebrates but indeed encourages business involvement within social development? Why not look for social return on investment partnered with financial return on investment when planning corporate programs?

Given the breadth of resources and strength of dynamism wielded by the private sphere, there exists incredible potential for significant social impact in conjunction with enhanced shareholder returns.

It is worth returning to the case of BHP Billiton in Mozambique. Why would a multi-national corporation, a profit-driven enterprise such as this, involve itself with the social issues faced by a poor African country?

Simply, because the success of its program not only improved community health, but also reduced absenteeism in the workforce from 22% to 2%. Measuring the improved productivity established the long term viability of the project. Downstream measuring of financial impact is key.

In many instances, social return may work in conjunction with achieving a commercial return when measured. This measurement is an innovative and emergent new space. Australian resource companies are amongst the global leaders in this space.

Do Australian companies that cut their teeth learning lessons of inter-cultural workings in indigenous communities have an unexploited comparative advantage in expanding work into developing economies?

Part Two: The Future for Australia.

A: VISION AND POLITICS

Do We Value Australia's Everyday Strengths?

Introduction

When I returned to Australia in late 2009 after living in many third world countries, I came to the view that Australia does not value her strengths. In 2010 I wrote this article.

Multimedia (ebook only)

There is a video on this theme 'Australia's golden age, an extract from the Richard Searby Oration *here*.

When I was being interviewed for the role of CEO of the Committee for Melbourne I was asked by the board "what do you like about Melbourne and why do you want to come home?"

My answer was simple. I said two things.

"You can drink water from the tap and you have the MCG."

Whilst the board thought I was being a bit flippant let's look at this. The fact that one can drink water from the tap says a lot about Melbourne's infrastructure. 80% of people on this planet can't drink water from the tap. If you can you are in the wealthiest 20% of people in the world. This very simple act, that we take for granted, says a lot about how much of our country works. There really are not many cities in the world where you can drink fresh clean and tasty water from the tap.

I consider this to be an enormous luxury. It is why when I go to a restaurant or cafe I refuse to buy bottled water. Why pay for water to come from the other side of the world with all of the greenhouse emissions in ignorance of what comes out of our tap?

And the MCG. We take that great icon for granted. Think about this: where else in the world can the family still afford to go to a major stadium and 100,000 people and get home safely without any flares rights for violence?

In North America is too expensive for a family to go.

In Europe it is too dangerous and the crowds are segregated by supporter base and you often see rights flares and violence.

Where else in the world to 12, 13 or 14-year-old girl say to their parents "hi Mum, I don't, I'm going to a mass public event with 100,000 people and no adult supervision" and Mum says "see you when you get home dear"?

Next time you go to the MCG have a look after the game at the number of 12, 13 and 14-year-olds in groups unsupervised. Ask yourself where else in the world could this happen?

When I was at the MCG for the 2010 grand final replay around about halfway through the final quarter I turned to my two brothers and said "boys, suck this up. This is about as good as the world gets. Here we are in a massive stadium with 100,000 people enjoying a game and there is no hint of violence and there is a sense of collective enjoyment. And above all our team is winning! This is as good as life gets".

Because we have such a failure to recognise what we are good at, we have a failure to recognise what is good. Because we don't celebrate success in individuals, we fail to see success as a society. This is why I also wrote a blog on the dangers of the Tall Poppy Syndrome.

Ours is an excellent society and we should celebrate excellence not hide from behind platitudes like words "lucky".

Was Occupy Melbourne right?

Introduction

With the 'Occupy' movement spreading across the world, Melbourne also had its own 'Occupy' largely following the principles of Occupy Wall Street. In 2011 I raised the question that given the fundamental differences in the economies and cultures of Australia and the United States, was it right for Occupy Melbourne to blindly follow Occupy Wall Street?

Wealth is a comparative notion and most people compare themselves with people close by, not those overseas. Someone who is in the wealthiest 2% of people on the planet will feel poor if they only look at the top 1%.

Take the Occupy Movement protesters. They love to say they are the 99%. Perhaps some are in the bottom 99% within Australia, but what about on a global scale? 80% of people on the planet do not have regular access to both electricity and water. The majority of people do not complete primary let alone secondary education. Almost no-one completes tertiary education. If one has, they are in the top 1% of people in the world - merely by starting tertiary education. On a global scale, most of the Occupy Movement protesters have the level of wealth and education that puts them in the top 1%!

We fail to look around us and recognise that here, in Australia, we have created a society that, according to outside assessors, is amongst the best, if not the best, form of life in all of human existence.

You do not hear the Occupy Melbourne people saying this.

It is interesting to look at recent data. The old saying of 'the rich are getting richer and the poor are getting poorer' is simply not true. In each of the OECD countries since 1980 the rich have been getting richer but the poor have been getting richer as well. Israel is an exception. Their poor have been getting poorer. It is true that the rich have been getting richer faster than the poor have been getting richer. This wealth disparity is something that needs to be examined and checked.

In Australia the top 10% have become wealthier by 4.5% per year since 1980, and the lower 10% have been getting richer at 3% per annum since 1980. One may be tempted to look at the disparity and not see two other interesting issues.

Firstly, the rate at which Australian lower 10% have been getting wealthier far exceeds the lower 10% in other OECD countries. Three per cent is a very good growth rate. In each of the other OECD countries, the bottom 10% has become richer on average by less than 1%. The lower 10% in Australia have been doing more than three times better than lower 10% of other OECD countries. This is an interesting comparative success.

What is even more interesting is that the top 10% of other OECD countries have increased their wealth at a rate of around about 2% per annum. The lower 10% of Australians have improved their wealth at a rate faster than the wealthiest 10% of OECD countries! Australia's poor have been getting richer faster than the rich in other OECD countries. This is remarkable.

Whilst we should continue to strive to improve our wealth disparity, surely we should be sitting back and celebrating this remarkable point about Australia: that our poor are getting richer faster than other countries rich are getting richer. But our country finds this so hard to believe that we neither celebrate it, nor analyse it and ask: how do we do even better still?

The Occupy Melbourne protesters mindlessly copied Occupy Wall Street (OWS), without really asking if the same conditions apply in Australia. On their 'We are the 99%' page, OWS say:

"We are the 99%. We are getting kicked out of our homes. We are forced to choose between groceries and rent. We are denied quality medical care. We are suffering from environmental pollution. We are working long hours for little pay and no rights, if we're working at all. We are getting nothing while the other 1% is getting everything. We are the 99%."

Let's critically examine each point as it applies to Australia:

1. *We are the 99%.* I pointed out earlier that on a global measure, most in Australia are in fact in the global 1%. This arguably does not apply in Australia.

2. *We are getting kicked out of our homes:* Australia does not have the foreclosures that apply in the United States. This point does not apply in Australia.

3. *We are forced to choose between groceries and rent.* There are a comparatively small number of Australians that are faced with this choice. Few countries in the world have as low rate of poverty as Australia. For those who need assistance, we need to help them more.

4. *We are denied quality medical care.* This does not apply in Australia. The system of Medicare still provides universal basic coverage. Medicare can be better, but no one suffers lack of medical to the degree that happens in the United States.

5. *We are suffering from environmental pollution.* To a degree yes. We have a good community movement to protest against environmental challenges, and we need to ensure this continues.

6. *We are working long hours for little pay and no rights.* Fair Work Australia, the award system and our comparatively high minimum wage puts Australia ahead of the United States. In the US, Federal adult minimum wage is $7.25 per hour. In Australia it is $10.59 at 18 rising to $15.15 at the age of 20. Many awards have a higher minimum. A 20 year old minimum wage in Australia is more than twice that of the US. Whilst I am not saying Australia is perfect, I am saying that it is far better placed than the US.

7. *...if we're working at all.* Australian unemployment is close to what economists call 'full employment'. In the US it is approaching 10%

I am not saying Australia is perfect, far from it. I am however saying that Australia is in a far better position than arguably every other nation in the world. Rather than blindly copying protests from overseas, I believe we should lead a discussion fully examining our strengths and weakness and build on these strengths while reducing the weaknesses. Australia does not need to fundamentally change its system, but it does need to fine tune the system. To fine tune the system we need to understand our strengths.

Bi-partisan liberalism

Introduction

The major political parties based on employer versus employee no longer represent the conservative versus progressive division in Australia, or so I wrote in this 2011 opinion article.

Multimedia (ebook only)
This article bears close resemblance to views published nearly a decade earlier <u>here</u>.

For most of the last 100 years the ideological framework in Australian politics has been one of worker versus employer. The workers and their supporters looked to the ALP, and the employers and their supporters looked to the Liberal Party. This was the framework of Australian politics for generations.

The shrinking union membership shows that Australian's have changed even if politics has not.

The Labor Party platform until a few years ago had within it the 'socialist objective' that called for the nationalization of industry to the extent necessary to limit the exploitation of the workforce.

This framework had been out of date for some time when it was removed. The economic, legal and social tools available to government had created many other ways to limit exploitation than just the heavy hand of nationalization.

With decreasing unionism and the creation of other tools, many more debates in Australia are about general equity, fairness and social justice.

But social justice doesn't belong just to the labour movement.

The philosophical liberalist tradition is about the freedom for people to attain their potential within a community while recognizing the need to look after those in genuine need. Liberalism can claim an interest in social justice too, not just those in the Labor Party.

But in Australia when one talks of liberalism, one immediately thinks of the Liberal Party. There is confusion between the name of the party and the name of the philosophical tradition.

The problem is that the Liberal Party a conservative party and not a liberal one.

How does this play out in Australian politics today? Let's look at some issues.

Take gay marriage. Under a liberalist philosophical tradition there would be sympathy for gay marriage. Under a conservative political tradition there would not. So what of the Liberal Party?

The current conservative leaning leadership has the Liberal Party objecting to gay marriage, even though many so called 'wets' from a liberal philosophical tradition would like to support the change. The Liberal Party is split along a conservative versus progressive divide.

Same in the Labor Party.

Many in the religious right of the Labor Party – especially from the catholic union base of the SDA union - oppose the gay marriage changes.

On the other hand many from a social justice but non-union background in the Labor Party support gay marriage.

You therefore have two unusual alliances forming within parliament: The pro-gay marriage camp from both the social justice (non-Catholic Labor Party) and liberalist (Wet Liberal Party) on one hand and the anti-gay marriage from the catholic Labor and Conservative Liberal sides.

Anti-gay marriage is made up of some Labor and some Liberal. Pro-gay marriage is made up of some Labor and some Liberal also. What does this mean for party politics?

There are many in the Labor Party who come from a non-unionist background but who joined the party on the basis of a belief in social justice. They are not so interested in the worker versus employer divide of the cold war days, but they are interested in social justice.

There are those in the Liberal Party who are philosophically also interested in social justice not the employer verses employee divide. So who to support or vote for?

When asking oneself which party to support, one cannot look at the moderates of the two parties as they are too similar to differentiate. One needs to look at the extremes of the parties and see which you are least uncomfortable with.

Let's take asylum. You used to be able to say that Labor was too easy and Liberal too harsh. Now they are the same.

I do not believe any of the three parties have the policy settings right on asylum, but I see so little difference between the Labor and Liberal Party positions, and see both parties' language based on the same fear and hatred, that the social justice part of me cannot accept either party.

Likewise the social justice part cannot accept a policy that would encourage people to get on leaky boats.

I, like many Australians, am disillusioned at politics. I feel the Labor/Liberal divide no longer represents the ideological difference that exists in Australia today.

I no longer think the divide is Union or Boss, I believe Australia more debates conservative politics and liberalist politics of social justice. The problem is there are Conservatives in both the Liberal Party and Labor Party. There are social justice-liberals in both the Labor Party and Liberal Party.

Parties no longer debate different belief, they just debate power. They don't inspire us to follow them; they try and scare us about the other side.

No wonder people are confused. The truth is we don't need just new leaders of the two political parties. It is not about changing Abbott or Gillard. What we need is: new parties. We need a conservative Party and a Progressive Party so Australians get to choose on belief, not personality. Perhaps then we might get better government.

Time to fund our Consuls better.

My younger brother died recently in Bali. He had been living there for four years. He had built a clothing brand from scratch and was gaining good sales through his physical shops and online store before his life was unexpectedly cut short at the age of 37.

He is not alone. An Australian is said to die in Bali every nine days.

Australians are great travellers, but one downside of travel is that catastrophe can strike a family when it is least expected. There is no greater visible tragedy than the face of a parent bidding their final good bye to a child.

When a death takes place in another country the tragedy can be exacerbated by the unfamiliarity a grieving family may have with the differing processes and cultures.

Indonesia, with a different legal and health system, together with additional diplomatic and quarantine issues that Australian authorities require for the return of remains, provides additional complications.

Added to that are simple practical issues that arise when heading overseas to retrieve a fallen loved one. Where does a family get a car and driver who can guide you to the police station, hospital, morgue, crematorium and other places that are not on a tourist route? How do you get local telephones to stay in touch with each other and families back home with out being hit by exorbitant roaming charges?

How do you explain the system of autopsies in Indonesia to Australians who may not realise that it is normal for a family to pay up front for that autopsy? I stress here that I am not saying Australia has a better or worse system than Indonesia. I am just saying the systems are different.

Grief is not a good state of mind in which to navigate cultural, linguistic and legal differences. The heightened emotion of grief can lead to missteps or misunderstandings by families dealing in the different culture and system that may inadvertently lengthen the process of releasing personal possessions and remains.

Our family was more prepared than some when dealing with our loss. My brother had a deep and strong friendship group in

Bali who dropped everything to help us. A friend who accompanied our family knew Indonesia well and spoke a little Indonesian.

I had previously been a senior United Nations official in conflict and natural disaster settings and had dealt with many governments and cultures in difficult situations. My father at one point had been one of Victoria's coroners. We were as prepared as a family can be for an unexpected tragedy.

Other families are not in this position.

What happens to the families of the other Australians? Around 40 families each year make the sorrowful trek to Bali if there were no strong local friendship group or without deep experience in navigating different legal and political systems? Where would a family even begin the navigation of a difficult system without help in knowing where they need to start?

We found the Indonesian police and medical services to be empathetic, caring and open to sharing information on what was an unclear situation. But while many of them can speak better English than the average Australian speaks Indonesian, misunderstandings in language always occur.

One may think that one of the roles of the Australian Consulate staff in places like Bali would be to help Australian families with such issues. Our experience with Australian Consulate staff in Bali was a good one and we remain grateful to them. Caring and loving staff empathised and helped as much as they could.

Alas funds for diplomatic posts are scarce and getting scarcer. Consulate staff wish to help families like ours. However they find resource constraints mean they are limited in the assistance they can offer.

With so many Australians heading to places like Bali and Phuket, sheer weight of numbers dictates that more Australians are at risk. Families need to head to these places to deal with consequences of accidents, misadventures or crime that may have see a travelling teenager, or expatriate worker, unexpectedly lose their life.

For those families that may not have as much support as we did, or our unusual working experience to call upon, more funding

110

needs to be provided so extra assistance can be given by Australian Consular staff.

Certain consulate posts around the world should have greater funding and a larger mandate to help grieving Australians. Diplomatic posts outside of the common law legal system where English is not the mother tongue and where many Australians visit, should be high on this list for additional support.

With the visitor numbers in places like Bali, we should start there.

We as a country should recognise the enormous grief that many or our compatriot families go through. When this happens overseas we should do more as a country to ease that pain. The next family could be yours.

Is The Tall Poppy Syndrome is Killing Australia

Introduction

In the Richard Searby Oration I spoke of Australia's new "golden age". I find that sometimes the 'Tall Poppy Syndrome' is killing Australia.

Australians are a perverse lot.

The fact that we have been recognised as the second most liveable country in the world and Melbourne the world's most liveable city, should give us cause to celebrate. We somehow cringe at these titles.

What is it about the tall poppy syndrome that stops us from celebrating success? We do not, in this culture, allow people to celebrate what they are good at. If they did, we would tell them that they are "full of themselves", or, "up themselves".

We have perhaps taken our egalitarian nature, which is essentially good, to a level that it is doing us harm. It is doing us harm because the egalitarian nature and the tall poppy syndrome in preventing us from celebrating success does three things:

1. It forces people with high ambition to either hide the ambition or reduce the ambition.

2. Perhaps worse, it stops us from celebrating the success and enjoying today for the things that we have done well.

3. When we have done something well we like to look for an external cause such as "luck".

Let me give you three examples to demonstrate each of the above points.

When incredibly successful Australians return from overseas rather than celebrating their stories for their friends and families often wish that they do not speak too much of their success. They are encouraged to keep those stories to themselves. But you do not even have to be incredibly successful to have pressure to keep silent.

A good friend of mine has been a nanny in Europe for the last 15 years. She is a very good nanny. She works for some of the wealthiest families in Europe which means they are normal working week would have in London for two days, Geneva for three days in Paris for two days each week.

When she first came home to Australia and people asked her "what is your normal work week" and she answered with your travel plans she very quickly got the impression that people thought she was full of herself, merely because she travelled to 3 exotic cities every week.

People did not look behind the reality of each of the cities being a mere one hour flight from each other. It was like her saying that she spent two days each week in Melbourne, three in Adelaide and two in Sydney. If she said this, people would just think that is a normal Australian life for a job that requires travel.

But because she had been in Europe, and the cities were somehow exotic, she quickly learned to tell boring stories, because she would be criticised too much for talking about what she actually did do.

Australians also find hard to believe that we are the world's most liveable city in the world's second most liveable country. We fail to look around us and recognise that here, in Australia, we have created a society that according to outside assessors is amongst the best, if not the best form of life in all of human existence.

You do not hear the Occupy Melbourne people saying this.

It is interesting to look at recent data. The old saying of the rich are getting richer and the poor are getting poorer is simply not true. In each of the OECD countries since 1980 the rich have been getting richer but the poor have been getting richer as well. It is true that the rich have been getting richer faster than the poor have been getting richer in each of the countries and this wealth disparity is something that needs to be examined and checked.

In Australia the top 10% have become wealthier by 4.5% per year since 1980, and the lower 10% have been getting richer at 3% per annum since 1980.

But it is interesting to look at the rate at which Australian lower 10% have been getting wealthier. Three% is a very good growth rate. Indeed in each of the other only CD countries in the bottom 10% have become richer on average by about 1%. The lower 10% in Australia have been doing much better than lower 10% of other OECD countries.

What is even more interesting is that the top 10% of other OECD countries have increased their wealth at a rate of around about two% per annum. The lower 10% of Australians have improved their wealth at a rate faster than the wealthiest 10% of OECD countries.

Not only have the top 10% in Australia been getting richer faster than the rest of the OECD world, but our bottom 10% has also become richer faster than the rich in the rest of the world.

Whilst we should continue to strive to improve our wealth disparity, surely we should be sitting back and celebrating this remarkable point about Australia: that our poor are getting richer faster than other countries rich are getting richer.

But we find this hard to believe. It is a bit like Australia saying that we escaped the Global Financial Crisis because of the mining sector. This is too simplistic. It gives us an ability to simply say we were "lucky".

Why cannot we recognise that in escaping the global financial crisis we are seeing the culmination of three decades of very good policy across all political parties? What saved us from the GFC was a combination of a flexible exchange rate (thanks to Hawke and Keating) a flexible labour market (thanks to Howard and Costello), a strong and well regulated banking sector that has not collapsed (two in Australia would look to our four banks as saviours?) and, yes in part, the mining sector.

Whilst we are lucky with our resources, the other three factors were a result of good planning. Why don't we celebrate this?

When I was being interviewed for the role of CEO of the Committee for Melbourne I was asked by the board "what do you like about Melbourne and why do you want to come home?"

My answer was simple in that I said two things.

"You can drink water from the tap and you have the MCG."

Whilst the board thought I was being a bit flippant let's look at this. The fact that you can drink water from the tap says a lot about our infrastructure. 80% of people on this planet can't drink water from the tap. If you can you are in the wealthiest 20% of people in the world. This very simple act, that we take for granted, says a lot about how much of our country works. There really are not many cities in the world where you can drink fresh clean and tasty water from the tap.

I consider this to be an enormous luxury. It is why when I go to a restaurant or cafe I refuse to buy bottled water. Why pay for water to come from the other side of the world with all of the greenhouse emissions in ignorance of what comes out of our tap?

And the MCG. We take that great icon for granted. Think about this: where else in the world can the family still afford to go to a major stadium and 100,000 people and get home safely without any flares rights for violence?

In North America is too expensive for a family to go.

In Europe it is too dangerous and the crowds are segregated by supporter base and you often see rights flares and violence.

Where else in the world to 12, 13 or 14-year-old girl say to their parents "hi Mum, I don't, I'm going to a mass public event with 100,000 people and no adult supervision" and Mum says "see you when you get home dear"?

Next time you go to the MCG have a look after the game at the number of 12, 13 and 14-year-olds in groups unsupervised. Ask yourself where else in the world could this happen?

When I was at the MCG for the 2010 grand final replay around about halfway through the final quarter I turned to my two brothers and said "boys, suck this up. This is about as good as the world gets. Here we are in a massive stadium with 100,000 people enjoying a game and there is no hint of violence and there is a sense of collective enjoyment. And above all our team is winning! This is as good as life gets".

Because we have such a failure to recognise what we are good at we have a failure to recognise what is good. Because we don't celebrate success in individuals we fail to see success as a society.

Ours is an excellent society that we should celebrate, not hide from behind platitudes like words "lucky".

The greatest threat to us is complacency that comes from not recognising how good we are and therefore not fighting hard enough to protect. Australia is in a very good position to maximise the next half a century but our greatest threat is in not recognising what a good position we are in.

Australia: Informed and hopeful or ignorant and fearful?

Introduction

I write this article as an Australian, and in a personal capacity based on both my background as an international lawyer and of having worked for the United Nations High Commission for Refugees, the International Committee of the Red Cross, and other agencies in some of the world's most atrocious of circumstances.

Multimedia (ebook only)

There is a video on this theme 'Australia's golden age, an extract from the Richard Searby Oration *here*.

Two of the greatest threats we have in this country today are ignorance and fear. Ignorance of change that will naturally happen, and fear of that very same change. Globalisation, population, demographic changes and continued multiculturalism a visible components in this on-going change.

Fear of this change can manifest itself in many ways with some of the fear manifested in our refugee debate.

Conversely the greatest opportunities for Australia derive from us being informed and hopeful. Informed about the opportunities the future brings, and hopeful about the change that will result.

If I were PM I would want Australians 'informed and hopeful' even more than 'relaxed and comfortable'. I would certainly want them to be 'informed and hopeful' rather than 'ignorant and fearful'.

Surely this is the great challenge for leadership in this country – to lead on hope, not lead on fear? It is a sad truism in politics that it is easier to preach fear, hatred and intolerance, on one hand, than it is to preach compassion understanding and tolerance on the other.

Our leaders' challenge is to break that truism and the challenge exists equally for PM, Opposition leader and minor parties. Whilst we have seen the PM's narrative turn positive in many areas, although sadly not on asylum issues, the same change is yet to start in the camp of the Opposition Leader.

I want Australians to be informed and hopeful around all issues, but particularly around asylum seekers and refugees. I have written more on the 'Carrots and Sticks' below that could provide a better refugee solution - one that helps not hinders our international reputation.

Many can mount an argument about the horrors faced by refugees and why Australia should do the right thing in accepting refugees. But it is an argument that sadly lacks traction in today's Australia.

The argument for humanity lacks traction in Australia because we allowed some sectors of our community to take the fear I referred to, and turn it into hatred.

As a community, we failed to stop the genie leaving the bottle when we were tempted with the Tampa.

The time has come for us to fight the genie.

I would suggest three things:

- Firstly we must urgently change our national narrative from one based on negative to one based on positive, not just to asylum and refugee policy, but to a whole raft of policies. Our current national debate does us no good. Our current national debate is causing us brand image harm. Our current national debate is setting us up to be the future regional cringe not the future regional hinge.

- Secondly, we must change our dialogue on asylum from that of location of processing to how we handle resettlement regardless of where that processing takes place. Any discussion on resettlement must be handled regionally and the Bali process is a good place for that to start.

- Thirdly, it is in my view no longer good enough policy-makers to say "I am quietly raising these issues within my party room but I cannot speak out in public". Because this issue is an issue that is move beyond that of boats, because it is an issue that has moved beyond that of even people, because it is an issue that has become one about the "content of our national character", it is no longer good enough to quietly change things from the inside if they are yielding so painfully to change. You must speak out publicly.

Australia is a good country. It is a nation of well-meaning people. It is a nation of people with a good heart. But it is a truism in a democracy that if you have the chance of preaching fear hatred and intolerance on one hand and compassion togetherness and understanding on the other, fear hatred and intolerance wins almost all the time.

This is that reason that we believe people like Nelson Mandela are rare, precisely because they chose the difficult task of preaching compassion togetherness and understanding.

I believe for this country Tampa was a turning point. I believe Tampa was the time that we legitimised fear as a genuine political tactic in our country.

We urgently must work to put the genie back in the bottle; we must reverse our national psyche of negativity and create a dialogue of the positive for after all, that is what this country should be.

We have a lot of fear in our country, but what is not fear, is hope.

People like me will help but at the end of the day – it is up to you.

Time to make Australia Positive Again.

Introduction

Australians are growing more and more tired of the negativity of our political debate. I know I certainly am.

Instead of being positive, our politicians are negative. In 2011 I spent a lot of time challenging people to be positive instead of negative.

Multimedia (ebook only)

An edited version appeared in the Herald Sun here. In addition I spoke of how Australia could be in its Golden Age here as part of the Richard Searby Oration in 2011.

Refugees, carbon tax, population growth, are all issues of importance, but we as Australians are being asked more often than not to choose between alternative views of fear, not hope. We are being asked more often than not to vote against something we fear, not for something we want.

Australians are tiring of fear and negativity from whichever side it may come. Australians would like to hear some inspiration, and hear how our country can be lead based on a vision of a good future. We are a good country and continue to be the lucky country, hence it is time both our political leaders gave us this hope and optimism.

Here is the speech I would love to hear a PM or an Opposition Leader give. I am not saying this should be Julie Gillard, or Tony Abbott, rather a hypothetical 'future political leader'. It would run something like this:

"Australians, we the parliament, have heard you. You are tired of negativity; tired of the school yard fighting that is question time. You are tired of fear and thirst for inspiration.

We hope you will see it is a sign of good leadership to admit mistakes and change course when change is needed.

We were wrong to inspire fear. We were wrong to dress things in the negative. We are wrong to demonize our political opponents. Our opponents may well have a different perspective on where our country should head, but we must recognise that both Government and Opposition MPs have the best intentions in mind for Australia. They may have a different view on how to get there, but there intention is good.

We must recognise areas where our policy views converge, and areas where our views diverge. It is our responsibility as both government and opposition to construct a positive debate around those areas of divergence to give Australians a clear decision of alternative government policies based on hope not fear – opportunity not threat.

It is time to hit the national 're-set button'. It is time for a dialogue to be one of hope.

And let's start our discussions from the point of strength that we now have. Our growth was 1.2% last quarter. Greece: negative7%. Our unemployment is 5.2%; The US nearing 10.

Australia is in the ideal future time zone. We are geographically at the critical point of the globe. With our ethnic mix as one of the most multi-cultural nations on earth, we are ideally placed to be the interface hinge between the Anglo-Saxon and Asian worlds.

This should be our Golden Time. Despite current equity market turmoil, this should be the time where we debate a bright future. Our choices should be ones of inspiration and if this is to be the Asian Century, we should be the century's cultural hinge, not cultural cringe.

Let's start the national reset with asylum seekers.

Many have said that the refugee issue should not be a big issue. And I agree. It should not be. But it is.

This issue has now moved beyond one of boats. It has moved beyond the location of processing. It has even moved beyond one of people.

This has grown now to become an issue about the soul of our country, an issue about the content of our collective character. It is now a debate about who we are and how we wish to be perceived.

Whatever we decide as policy, we should aim to enhance and not detract from our country's international reputation with our debate on alternative policy solutions.

We are an intelligent country that can engage in difficult debate and we should not debate in sound bites. The asylum debate is difficult and it does our country no good to simply say 'stop the boats'. But nor does it do justice to a complicated issue to say 'just let them land'. We need to find a way to engage the community in a deep and detailed dialogue on a complicated issue.

We have in this country been debating the wrong issue. The location of processing – Australia, Malaysia or Nauru is the wrong discussion. The harder and more critical issue is that of resettlement once a refugee is processed. If you fix the resettlement issue, people will not even get on boats.

But resettlement is tough as it involves all countries in our region agreeing on what their 'fair share' of the asylum seekers is. PNG's fair share. Nauru's fair share. New Zealand's fair share. Indonesia's fair share. Our fair share.

Our policy should be about who comes to our country and the circumstances in which they come, not a policy on who we stop from coming to our country and the circumstances in which we stop them.

Ours should be a 'controlled entry policy' not a 'Border Protection' policy. It should be regional and one based on the opportunities we have to strengthen regional alliances, and the opportunities that come from a continued broad mix of our national ethnic make-up.

This is but one example. This is where we start.

We can and must 'Make Australia Positive Again'."

That is the Speech I would like to hear and I would vote for whichever party leader who would give it.

A challenging time for Labor too.

Introduction

Following the 2001 election, the Federal Labor Party had to debate again the role of asylum seekers in its policy platform. As it turned out the issue has outlived the Democrats as a party, Gillard as immigration Shadow Minister and still haunts her Prime Ministership. This article was published in 2002, but is still relevant a decade later, as my *Bi-Partisan Liberalism* article showed (see previous chapter).

Whilst some commentators have written off the Democrats following the divisive personality 'train wreck' of recent times, the Democrats' trouble may also put sharper focus on the deepening divisions in the ALP.

Labor's recent turmoil has revolved around the so-called 60/40 rule - the rule that determines the percentage of Union versus rank and file membership at party conferences. Regardless of union representation being 60/40 or 50/50, there is still roughly half the membership of the party that is made up of the 'rank and file' for whom 'collective bargaining' may not be the leading issue.

When one removes a belief in collective bargaining as an appropriate mechanism in the industrial relations system from a political discussion, a yawning question remains: Why did the other half of the party chose the ALP over the Liberal Party or Democrats as a political voice for them?

If the Democrats existed to 'keep the bastards honest' – what is the Labor Party's claim to those outside the union movement? Could they jump to a reinvigorated and renewed 'Liberal Democrat' party?

Ask a non-union ALP member why they joined and the majority of the responses will include a belief in compassion, tolerance, social justice and the like. You may even get a discussion on a belief in Social Democracy or Democratic Socialism.

You may even get members harking back to the ideals of former leaders like Doc Evatt. Of his negotiations in the lead up to creation of the UN Doc Evatt said:

"It only amounts to recognising a duty of decency towards helpless people. If the Labour Movement does not stand for that, it does not deserve to exist."

Chifley's 'Light on the Hill' speech is one that inspires ALP members and beseeches them to search out and assist people in need wherever they may be found.

Paul Keating's 'True Believers' speech warned of the dangers of a coalition government – particularly the lack of tolerance he thought a coalition would bring – and a withdrawal from a role of helping others on the international stage.

And now many in the ALP rank and file are questioning their belief in the ALP principally as they feel the ALP failed to measure up to its own standards over the refugee and asylum issues.

Many though have stayed true. They recognised the difficult political position the party was placed in by a canny Howard – yet their steadfastness is temporary awaiting final policy determination from the ALP.

This is one of Julia Gillard's great tests in reshaping Labor's Asylum policy.

She must come up with a policy that is true to the ALP's fundamental core beliefs of compassion, tolerance and equity. One that seeks out to assist people in need   - one that falls back on Evatt's claim that 'it only amounts to recognising a duty of decency towards helpless people.'

For if Gillard cannot do that within the political realities of the time then many members may turn back to Evatt's other comment: "If the Labour Movement does not stand for that, it does not deserve to exist" – or that it does not deserve their membership.

Enter the Democrats.

The Democrats are now re-examining their reason to exist – indeed they may split with the 'Gang of Four' going one way, and Natasha's people going the other way. This may be the last act of the destruction of the Democrats, or it could reshape them into a major political power, filling the vacuum that now exists in Australia.

There is now a major place for Liberal Party supporters who are social and economic liberals (read progressive) and moderate ALP members for whom social democracy as a concept is more important than a sole focus on collective bargaining.

Both of these groups feel let down by their parties shift to the populist right, but as yet they have nowhere to jump.

What if the Democrats could use the recent disasters to rename and reshape the political framework?

What if they could recover the real beliefs of liberalism – compassion, tolerance, and the tempering of economic progress by recognition of the need to continually narrow the gap between rich and poor.

So to return to Ms Gillard. If the Asylum seeker policy she eventually releases is not driven primarily by compassion and tolerance then many ALP members could be looking to exit permanently – and a reinvigorated and united Australian Democrats could just provide them with a new more comfortable home

Why I quit the Labor Party

Introduction

After 24 years a member of the ALP, standing for public office in a marginal seat, holding many branch office and policy positions, Andrew MacLeod quit the Labor Party. He proposes a new 'bi-partisan liberalism'. Here is why.

My father had been an active member of the Labor Party. In November 1975 I rode my bicycle around the streets with a 'We Want Gough' and a 'Shame Frazer Shame' badge pinned to my chest. I remember meeting Whitlam as a kid and being presented a Tonka toy for coming second in a sack race at the ALP family day at Bernley Oval in the mid 1970's.

Even though my family had a strong Labor background, my joining was not automatic. I took the time and made my own decision on which party to join. The choice came after deep thought.

In the end I summed up my reasoning thus: One can not look at the moderates of either political party for guidance on which to join, for they are too similar. One has to look at the radicals of the parties and decide which is least disconcerting.

Back in 1988 when I looked at the outliers of both parties I came to this conclusion: The Labor Party believed in having a social safety net a bit too high. There was some waste, but few genuine people missed out. The Liberal Party had the social safety net too low. Less waste, but some genuine people missed out.

For me, it was 'less bad' to have a little waste and no-one missing out, compared to less waste and genuine suffering. This was the generalisation I used all through my time as a member of the Party.

Having had a long career working for the UN and for the Red Cross in hell zones like Rwanda, Bosnia, Kosovo, Pakistan, Afghanistan and others, Australia's place in the world and how we treated those less well-off, became more important to me.

Issues around asylum and refugees are the main yard-sticks I use in judging Australian society and politics.

I was disgusted by the events around the Tampa and the 2001 election. I was deeply involved as a candidate in a marginal Victorian seat only just missing out on election. No matter how much John Howard seeks to re-write history and say the Tampa had little to do with the result, it did.

Labor tied itself in knots after 2001, losing focus on its position on asylum, and missing an opportunity to put alternative policies to the Australian people. It is an extremely complicated issue. To simple it is to say 'Stop the Boats', but also to simple it is to say 'Let Them Land'. The issue does not lend itself to slogans if one is to lead a well thought national debate.

After election in 2007 and again after Gillard took over, Labor had the chance to reset the debate and lead the Australian people in a genuine, well thought out dialogue around alternative policy, based on positivity not negativity. Labor could have 're-set' the national mood to one of 'how do we safely and securely control entry to genuine asylum seekers' instead of continuing a negative dialogue around 'how we stop illegal entry and excise territory from our migration zone'.

Labor failed to take this chance.

Hence, when my membership renewal form arrived in the post in 2011, I could not see the principled leadership I searched for. I could not see a new challenging of the Australian people on the issues that matter to me. I could not find a meaningful difference between Labor and Liberal. How therefore, in all conscience, could I remain in the party? I decided to quietly let my membership lapse.

So why speak out now? If the camel's back were not already broken, excising the mainland from the migration zone would have done it for me. This additional slap in the face to core beliefs of mine means that I no longer wish to leave the Party quietly.

The issue of asylum is now an issue that defines our national character. It sets the tone of how we wish to be perceived by ourselves and by others. I don't like the tone we as a nation are now setting.

I have had friends say that I have been disloyal to the party for leaving. But to me, loyalty is to principles first, Party second and leadership third, not the other way around. Many in the Labor Party appear to have forgotten this.

Liberal Party apparatchiks can not rejoice in another member leaving Labor. Labor's current dysfunction hides very similar issues going on inside the Liberal Party, not to mention the devious nature of Liberal's deception on asylum as well.

Social justice doesn't belong just to the labor movement and some in the Liberal Party know this.

The philosophical liberalist tradition is about freedom for people to attain their potential within a community, while recognizing the need to look after those in genuine need. This is why some in the Liberal Party also speak out about the current asylum debate.

When you have those in both parties who share a progressive view on asylum, and others in both parties who don't, you begin to see that the old 'worker v boss' divide that historically characterized the two parties, no longer seems to be the relevant differentiator on the social issues of today.

It is not just asylum where this divide is seen. Take gay marriage. Under a liberalist philosophical tradition there would be sympathy for gay marriage. Under a conservative political tradition there would not. So what of the Liberal Party?

The current conservative leaning leadership has the Liberal Party objecting to gay marriage, even though many so called 'wets' from a liberal philosophical tradition would like to support the change. The Liberal Party is split along a conservative versus progressive divide.

Same in the Labor Party.

Many in the religious right of the Labor Party – especially from the catholic union base of the SDA union - oppose the gay marriage changes.

On the other hand many from a social justice but non-union background in the Labor Party support gay marriage.

You therefore have two unusual alliances forming within parliament: The pro-gay marriage camp from both the social justice (non-catholic Labor Party) and liberalist (Wet Liberal Party) on one hand and the anti-gay marriage from the catholic Labor and Conservative Liberal sides.

Anti gay-marriage is made up of some Labor and some Liberal. Pro gay-marriage is made up of some Labor and some Liberal also. There is a similar divide on asylum and a whole raft of other issues. In a way Australia has elements of bi-partisan liberalism and bi-partisan conservatism opposing each other on social issues. Yet this progressive versus conservative divide is not represented in the parties and therefore not represented in political debate.

What does this mean for party politics?

There are many in the Labor Party who come from a non-unionist background but who joined the party on the basis of a belief in social justice. They are not so interested in the worker versus employer divide of the cold war days, but they are interested in social justice. There are those in the Liberal Party who are philosophically also interested in social justice and not the employer verses employee divide.

But this is not where our public political debate is. Parties no longer debate different belief, they just debate power. Neither major leader inspires us to follow them, they try and scare us about the other side.

No wonder people are confused. The truth is we don't need just new leaders of the two political parties. It is not about changing Abbott or Gillard. Perhaps what we need is two new parties?

How about a conservative party to represent the conservative side on gay marriage, asylum, or even the monarchy? Likewise a liberalist, progressive party to represent the other would be good.

If we do not have parties that represent the real ideological divide in our community, then where is our democracy? Where is our choice? Australians should get to choose on belief, not personality. Perhaps then we might get better government.

B: INDIGENOUS AFFAIRS, RACE AND RACISM

Protection must be color blind.

Introduction

I first published the following in The Age in July 2009 following a trial of an indigenous man accused of raping a 12 year old tribal girl. His defence: it is acceptable in his culture. What do you think?

Multimedia (ebook only)
  The original is published in The Age here.

The abuse experienced by many Aboriginal children raises questions about the role cultural issues play when it comes to safeguarding our most vulnerable.

FIFTY years ago my father, employed as a federal government patrol officer, removed from their parents Aboriginal children thought to be at risk of harm. Ten years ago I wrote an apology for that removal in The Age and called upon the Federal Government to do the same. Last year the Government finally did so.

Now the Productivity Commission tells us that Aboriginal children are six times more likely to suffer abuse than non-Aboriginal children. Last year an Aboriginal man claimed as part of his defence in a Queensland court that he saw nothing wrong in having sex with a 12-year old Aboriginal child as she "did it with everyone".

Yet if I were to call for that Aboriginal child to be removed from an environment in which it was felt that a 12-year-old girl having sex with an adult was OK, I would be accused of repeating the evils of the removals policy implemented by my father. Conversely, if I called for a 12-year-old white child in Melbourne to be left in an environment where she had sex with an adult, I would rightly be called perverted.

Where have we gone wrong? Let me make a couple of clear statements, and then look at some difficult issues.

If a child is at risk from the family environment, then the state should seriously examine the removal of that child regardless of the child's colour, race or religion. A child should never be left in an environment where he or she is susceptible to harm. These are easy statements to make, but how do we implement it?

When my father implemented removals of Aboriginal children in the late 1950s, his original papers show that he tried to do so with the best intentions of the child in mind. He tried to "remove them from harm". While policy implementation in the '50s had less of the racial overtones than removals of the 1930s, those racial overtones nevertheless remained. One of many big errors of the 1950s was that in determining "best interests" of the child or "harm" to the child, a European perspective was always used, not taking into account culture, identity and belonging.

So what do we do now for children at risk of "harm"? What is the culture that determines "right" and "wrong" in modern Australia — indigenous or otherwise?

Do we now have an "Australian cultural standard" that could help us determine "harm", "right" or "wrong" regardless of ethnic background? Can we use this standard to protect children regardless of race — or do we fear accusations of repeating past wrongs so much that we are frozen with inaction?

When I look up the word "indigenous" in the dictionary I find confusing alternatives. One definition says "of or from a place". I was born here, my father was born here, so was my grandmother. By that definition I am indigenous, but I am not Aboriginal. Another says "natural and not introduced". Well, as the cane toad was introduced, I suppose so was the white man. But regardless of my race, or heritage, I belong in Australia. I don't have anywhere else to go.

My culture is the culture of this country.

Australia's culture is a mix and harmony of so many cultures, from that of Tasmanian Aborigines that predated the arrival of the mainland Aborigines in the last Ice Age, who in turn predated the arrival of the white man, who predated the Chinese, who predated the Greeks, Italian, later the Vietnamese, and now many from other countries as well. But do we have a universal Australian "culture" to which we all belong? Do we want an Australian culture?

I have worked in many countries for the United Nations and the Red Cross. I have seen people fight each other in wars over relatively small cultural differences, be it the Serbs and the Croats, both of whom are southern Slavs, the Tutsis and Hutus in Rwanda, the Tamils and Sinhalese in Sri Lanka. I do not seek to dilute their cultures, but in my view more united them than divided them — yet they fought.

Now we in Australia have a challenge. Do we have a culture? Do we want a culture? Can this culture protect children? Or do we seek to differentiate ourselves in the name of protecting identity and history, be it Aboriginal tribes and peoples, newly arrived Islamic Australians, Irish, Italian, Greek, or my father at the Melbourne Scots in his kilt? Will we allow different cultural norms for different Australian communities, or the application of different laws to different races in the country as was practised in Australia before the referendum of the 1960s?

In my view each Aboriginal language that is lost to history is lost to me and my family as much as to indigenous communities. Each law lost through time, each cultural practice forgotten, is lost to me because it is lost to Australia and all her people, and I belong to her. I may have not been educated in the ways of all communities in this country, but all are part of me.

In the same way, all of Australia is part of each of us. It is time we say that with pride. It is time that we say, in the words of Bruce Woodley "I am, you are, we are Australian" and unashamedly say that our culture is a melting pot of many. Yet there is a fundamental minimum that we should not go below. And that fundamental minimum is the protection of children.

So, what is the "harm" that we protect children from? If my father's error of the 1950s was using a European cultural perspective when assessing harm, what cultural perspective should we use now? In some Aboriginal traditional cultures and laws, sex with a 12-year-old is acceptable, in others not. In European culture it is not.

Australia has another opportunity for us to debate who we are. The simple question of "when is a child at harm?" raises many more cultural issues that we must not only debate. It is a quandary we must solve.

Andrew Macleod is a Melbourne-born international lawyer who has worked for the Red Cross and the United Nations and whose own family was split by issues around the stolen generation.

It's not about the parrot.

When you get a joke by email from a friend, and it offends you, how to you respond? This was my approach in 2013.

A friend of mine sent me a joke by email. Let's call him 'Fred' (not his real name).

The email came with a photo of a pretty young Muslim girl wearing a pink head covering. She had a coloured parrot sitting on her shoulder. It was a wonderful picture.

Here is how the joke went:

"I was in a pet shop when I noticed a Muslim with the most amazingly coloured parrot perched on her shoulder.

"Where did you get that from?" I asked.

"Christmas Island, Australia,!!!...There are thousands of 'em!"

........said the Parrot."

In response I emailed 'Fred' saying that I found the joke offensive and not funny. He replied and apologised as he didn't intend to offend me.

While it is strong and courageous to apologise, he misses the point.

I didn't seek an apology. Rather I would have preferred a realisation that the 'joke' was wrong as in our society many don't see the harm 'jokes' like this can lead to.

In reply I asked 'Fred' to think back a few weeks to when the two French girls were yelled at on the bus in Melbourne see here.

I reminded 'Fred' that some bloody idiot thought it was somehow OK to abuse the French girls for the great crime of not speaking English. The Youtube commentators and international media asked not only why this yobbo yelled at the girls, they also rightly asked why no one on the bus came to their aid.

That is a good question. The abuse was bad, but a bus load of silent onlookers is perhaps even worse.

When failure to intervene becomes the norm, then abuse can get worse until you see things like commuters on an Indian bus remaining silent as a girl is raped. Silence is deadly over the long term.

I was a soldier once. In officer training we were taught moral courage and leadership. We were taught to look into our own hearts to know when things are right or wrong, when things are funny and when they are reinforcing stereotypes, or increasing hatred. We were taught to stand up when we see wrong being done.

I met 'Fred' during that Army training all those years ago. It is why we are still friends, and why I chose to take issue with him rather than just add his address to my spam filter. I said all of this to 'Fred' in a return email.

'Fred' is a grandfather now, so my email returned to the issue of the picture. The picture was pretty. Lovely girl. Probably a happy child.

But how would SHE feel knowing what her photo was used for, I asked Fred. How would 'Fred' feel if a photo of his granddaughter was circulated as the but of a joke?

I asked Fred how far we should let silence or consent continue? Is it ok to pass on a joke? Is it ok to stand by and watch someone bully a kid in the street if they were a Muslim? How would you feel if a big 'Aussie' bloke in the street yelled at a child and told her to take the headscarf off because it was 'un Australian'?

You think it wouldn't happen? Well ask the French girls how many people intervened to help them.

I still have faith that in his heart 'Fred' knows that a better thing to have done was to not send the 'joke'. I'm sure he just needed a reminder of the lesson from army training that we all need to start with our own actions – or inactions.

I chose to remind him of the lesson of army training those years ago because Fred had been a trainer back then, not a student. He was one of the people that taught me the very lesson he seemed to have forgotten.

I was curious to see where 'Fred's' email chain started so I scrolled down to see who initiated the 'joke'? Surprisingly, even though the joke mentions Australia, the email began in the UK, a country with a greater proportion of Muslims than ours.

The issue of staying silent is not an issue between friends or even an issue that is just in Australia. It is global and we are all connected. It's time we all stood up to vilification and to the tone of where our global society is heading – getting more polarised each day.

This becomes the point. We all know the old saying that all it takes for evil to triumph is when good men stay silent. But how many people stay silent now?

How many people reading this are thinking 'it was only a joke, don't get carried away', or 'what are you, the thought police'? How many people reading this article today have received 'jokes' like that and stayed silent, or worse still, hit the 'forward' button?

We must all ask ourselves where to draw our own line in the sand. Where does our moral courage start and finish? In the end this email exchange was not about Fred or my offence. It is about all of us. It is about where we choose to stand up, and when do we choose to stay silent.

Think about your response next time you receive an innocent 'joke' in your email box.

Has Multiculturalism worked?

Introduction
I had this article first published in edited form during 2011 in The Herald Sun. Many people say multiculturalism has not worked. Are they right?

Some may like to say multiculturalism in Australia has not worked. They are wrong.

Australia has nearly half its population either born overseas or with at least one parent born overseas. Whilst large proportions are from Europe, many are from Asia, South Asia, Africa and elsewhere.

Some of the oldest non-indigenous communities are the Afghanis and Chinese who arrived in the middle of the 18th century.

We are not only one of the oldest multicultural countries in the world; we are also one of the most multicultural countries in the world. According to surveys, Australia is the world's second most multicultural nation behind Luxemburg and equal with Switzerland – a land with four official languages and 22 Cantons.

Melbourne is the world's most liveable city and one of the most diverse and multicultural cities. Consider this:

- In 2006, 35.8% of its population was born overseas, exceeding the national average of 23.1%.
- In concordance with national data, Britain is the most commonly reported overseas place of birth, with 4.7%, followed by Italy (2.1%), Croatia (1.7%), Vietnam (1.6%), China (1.5%), and New Zealand (1.5%).
- Melbourne has the world's third largest Greek-speaking population after Athens and Thessaloniki (Melbourne's Greek sister city).
- The Vietnamese surname Nguyen is the second most common in Melbourne's phone book.[160]
- The city also features substantial Indian, Sri Lankan, and Malaysian-born communities, in addition to recent South African and Sudanese influxes.

- The cultural diversity is reflected in the city's restaurants serving various international cuisines.

So if multiculturalism does not work, then surely Australia would be rated as a poor quality country to live in and Melbourne a poor city?

Yet we see that Australia is ranked as the second most liveable country in the world, with Melbourne considered as the most liveable city in the entire world. The truth is that we are a welcoming and well-functioning multicultural country, with all countries but Norway lower in multiculturalism ranked below Australia in liveability.

Whilst it is true that we our society is not perfect, and we have moments of tension, like the Cronulla riots, these negatives are far outweighed by the positives we get from multiculturalism.

Australia must promote the benefits of our multicultural image if we are to maximise the benefits further.

A concrete example is the live beef exports. Rather than arguing with Indonesia about how they kill livestock, why doesn't Australia expand the Islamic halal abattoirs in Australia so we slaughter the beasts and sell the processed meat? We sell around $650 million worth of halal and kosher meat to around 40 regional countries already, so why not expand this?

Isn't it a new thought if we think of our multicultural population as an asset not a problem? Isn't it better to think of our multicultural population as a 'trade opportunity' not an 'Alan Jones threat'?

Moreover Australia has a once in a multi-generation opportunity to cement a golden future for years to come – if we get our national psych around multiculturalism right.

Australia could be the hinge point between the Anglo-Saxon worlds on the one hand, and the Asian and Islamic worlds on the other. Australia could not only be the geographic and time-zone hinge, our nation could also be the cultural translator that brings the old and new worlds together.

C: REFUGEES

Tampa, 12 months on.

Introduction

Having worked for the UN High Commission for Refugees this article is one in a series I published from 2000 through to 2011 lamenting the great shame of the paucity of Australian public debate. This was one of the earlier one, published in mid-2002.

Now that 12 months have passed since the Tampa 'crisis', we must look back less emotively at the issues surrounding Australia's refugee policy and where it has placed us, where it has placed the fraudulent asylum seekers and what we have done with the genuine refugees.

At the start we must recognise that boats of asylum seekers, like that intercepted by the Tampa, contain both genuine and disingenuous asylum seekers.

That said; if one sees a car accident on a lonely country road in which one person is obviously hurt, and one is obviously OK, most people would stop and help because one person *IS* hurt, not continue on because one is OK.

Likewise a boatload of asylum seekers should be treated as if the passengers are genuine, as some are, not treated as 'illegal' because of a few. Latter processing can sort out the real from the phoney.

If we are to treat asylum seekers properly then we must review a couple of questions that have been lost in the recent debate surrounding terms and conditions of detention.

Firstly we must remind ourselves of the conditions from which genuine refugees flee.

We must also re-examine the number of refugees that we consider to be our 'fair share' out of the 22 or so million people currently considered 'of interest' to the UNHCR.

To the first question: what are the conditions that genuine refugees flee from.

I cannot speak for all refugees - only speak of those that I have witnessed through work in 5 conflicts on 3 continents.

In Vojvodina, in northern Serbia, my work took me to a refugee orphanage in a town named Sombor – an orphanage that had been 'adopted' by the local Red Cross branch.

At this orphanage was a girl named Maria. She was 12 years old. Maria had fled the fighting in Bosnia. She had one day 'appeared' on the Croatia/Serbia border with a flood of refugees but without any family.

She said nothing. She did not speak. Something that happened to her or something she had seen caused her to close up, to shut her emotions in and let no emotion out.

Maria may not even be her real name, it was a name given to her at the orphanage, as her real name could not be coaxed from her.

On a warm night at a summer camp hosted for the refugee children by the Red Cross, the children laughed and played around the campfire. All of them did except Maria, who sat silently and alone under a tree.

And then, for no reason she stood and walked over me, sat, snuggled her head to my shoulder and cried.

What had she seen? What could have happened to her? Why would we turn our backs on people like her just because they arrive here by boat?

Why, if Maria arrived, would we lock her up in the desert?

Half a world away, in Rwanda, there are three sets of traffic lights. Beggar children gather at these lights hoping for a hand-out from some of the foreign workers.

I worked in Rwanda and one day stopped to share some toys with the kids. They each received a small and nearly worthless gift in monetary terms, but they all ran gleefully to play for the afternoon.

The next afternoon no beggar children were at the lights except one. The boy tapped on the vehicle window, leant in and handing Andrew a 20-franc coin (worth about one third of one cent) he said 'thank you sir' for the gift, and shared what little he had.

I carry that coin each day.

In our focus on 'illegal' we as a nation have forgotten about the 'genuine'. Genuine refugees have a right to come here, even by boat, even by people smugglers – even then they are not 'illegal'.

It is time that we as a nation remembered that on a lonely road we would stop and help an accident because someone *IS* hurt. Why then do we chastise and demonise asylum claims from the 'genuine' just because some amongst them are fraudulent?

Why do we as a Nation turn our backs on some in the greatest need, when at the same time a beggar boy feels the need to give, even when he has nothing to share?

Why is it that we as a wealthy nation even for an instant thought that 4,000 refugees out of 22 million was a 'flood' and a 'crisis'? What gives us the cheek to think that 4,000 would have been our 'fair share' out of 22 million, when Britain takes 100,000?

Not only were we wrong to turn our backs, not only are we wrong to detain children, we are wrong to think we have done anything like as much as we could or as much as we should.

For future policy alternatives the Labor choice is starker than for the Liberals. The famed 'Light on the Hill" speech that Laborites turn to for inspiration commands the Labor Party to seek out and search for those in need, *wherever they may be*. If it does not then it has no right to exist.

Stop the Bollocks

Introduction

Is 'Tony Gillard' trashing or representing the Australian reputation? Should we say 'Stop the Bollocks' instead of 'Stop the Boats'?

Multimedia (ebook only)

This article in an edited for was first published in The Herald Sun here on October 16 2011. I also spoke along similar lines in a speech here.

Few would disagree that the current debate around refugees, immigration and population is one of the poorest in Australian history. However, few realise that the bad image created by our leaders is also costing us Australian jobs.

Take international education. It is a sector in crisis. Glen Withers from Universities Australia has said that the way we frame the refugee and immigration debate has created an impression that Australia is unwelcoming to visitors and students.

Education is worth 1% of GDP to Australia and is a bigger expert earner than wheat, beef, gold or gas, yet an unwelcoming image turns away the foreigners that drive the jobs in this sector.

For every two international students Australia loses, our economy shrinks by a net extra job. The loss of 23,000 international students in 2011, and predictions of 75,000 by 2025, equals 11,500 jobs already and 37,500 jobs lost by 2015.

What about with tourism? We have seen a down turn and loss of jobs there too. Some is dollar related, but some is a growing reputation that we are unwelcoming.

I believe the unwelcoming reputation is wrong. But am I misguided on this? With more coverage on our refugee debate than our tourism ads, how do you think we are perceived?

Many have said that the refugee issue should not be a big issue. And I agree. It should not be. But it has now moved beyond one of boats, beyond the location of processing and moved beyond one of people.

This debate has grown to become an issue about the soul of our country, an issue about the content of our collective character.

It is now a debate about who we are and how we wish to be perceived.

The asylum debate is difficult and it does our country no good to simply say 'stop the boats'. But nor does it do justice to a complicated issue to say 'just let them land'.

We should be perceived as an intelligent country that should debate issues in details, and not sound bites.

While Hollywood may have been fascinated by 'Brangalina', the current race to the bottom of the barrel on refugee policy makes some think our Prime Minister's real name is 'Tony Gillard'. Neither of them is mapping out an optimistic or positive plan.

Perhaps we could start by changing the unwelcoming policy title from 'Border Control' to 'Controlled Entry'.

You can control entry with a positive or negative image. Boarder control implies we want to keep people away. Controlled entry implies we want people to come, albeit in an orderly manner. Perhaps then we can rescue our nation and make Australia positive again.

Raising Fear on Refugee Arrivals is a Red Herring

Introduction

Having worked for the UN High Commission for Refugees this article is one in a series I published from 2000 through to 2011 lamenting the great shame of the paucity of Australian public debate. This one from 2009.

Here we go again... a fear campaign about being swamped by refugees being ramped up by an unpopular leader searching for populist support.

Whilst there is a temptation to compare the Coalition's campaign of 2009 with the fear campaign of 2001, this year's effort is far more dangerous as it hides a bigger and more important issue than even 'Child Overboard'.

The issue is not 'Why are refugees coming to Australia' (we know why – Australia is a great beautiful and functioning country; who wouldn't want to come here?). The issue is 'Why are the refugees *leaving* Sri Lanka'.

Why are refugees leaving Sri Lanka when the war has *ended?* Why are people fleeing a 'peace'?

By raising the fear campaign about refugee arrivals, the Opposition is distracting us from asking 'What is Australia's role in stopping the departures?' Turnbull's campaign is stopping us from holding the government to account on the *real* issues. The Opposition is failing at their principle role.

'What is Australia doing to support the peace' is the real question hidden by a campaign from an unpopular Malcolm Turnbull seeking renewed support through populism.

The Australian Government, through the Australian Agency for International Development (AusAID) does support peace building programs all around the world. What are we doing in Sri Lanka?

As a fellow Commonwealth Country, but without the overtones of a former Colonial overlord, Australia has some moral sway in Sri Lanka – and additional sway attached to the financial investments AusAID makes in development. What is Australia doing with this influence?

Why isn't the Opposition pressing the government on these real issue rather than populism? Maybe the government is doing something, but we just don't know about it.

Whilst the Sri Lankan government can rightly be happy for succeeding in ending a war that lasted more than a quarter of a century, killing hundreds of thousands and spawning the invention of the 'Suicide Bomber', the Sri Lankans were told by many that winning the peace will be harder than winning the war.

The Sri Lankans have been told that in order to 'win the peace' the Tamils need to see a real 'peace dividend' with over-investment in infrastructure, economic development, education and social cohesion in the north of Sri Lanka where the Tamils are centred.

For a successful conclusion to the war and a winning of the peace the Sri Lankan Government has to establish to the Tamil people in the north that the benefits of a peace outweigh the costs of a war.

It is for this reason, in successful transitions from conflict to peace; smart governments tend to establish 'truth and reconciliation commissions' or something similar, leaving war crimes prosecutions for only the most severe of contraventions. The notion of retribution must be banished from the victor's mind-set, or the peace will fail.

So have the Sri Lankan's done this? Are they using the support – both moral and financial – of Government's like Australia in really seeking a peace dividend?

No.

Instead of peace and reconciliation we see a block by the Sri Lankan Government of western aid agencies and observers access to the conflict and Tamil zones. We hear fleeing Tamil's telling stories of horrific camp condition and retribution and we have no real independent evaluation.

The reason we even begin to have a refugee *arrival* in Australia, is because we have a refugee *departure* from Sri Lanka.

This lack of interest and investment in peace is the *real* problem, and our lack of knowledge on what Australia is or isn't doing to support the peace is because the media space is full of the xenophobic fear campaigns, rather than the smart and nuanced debate that an educated and smart Australian population deserve.

Whilst the debate around support to Indonesia's ability to control boats, or Australia's processing regime on Christmas Island has a genuine place in generalised discussions, the current influx of Tamil's seeking asylum because the war has ended in their homeland points to much more nuanced and much tougher questions for the Government. Unfortunately the Oppositions seem incapable of grasping this reality and unwilling to hold the government to account.

While a democratic system requires a responsive government, it also requires a responsible opposition, and on the refugee issue, the Opposition is failing to hold the government to account to the real issues, and is thereby failing the Australian people.

Are Abbott and Howard just like Milosevic?

In 1996 I met Slobodan Milosevic when I worked for
the International Committee of the Red Cross
in former Yugoslavia. His evil could be felt through his
handshake. The heart of his evil was his ability to put his own
political advancement and power before anything - even lives.

Milosevic ensured that Serb nationalism was revived in 1989
when on 28 June of that year one million Serbs went to 'the
Battlefield of the Blackbird's' at Gazimestan to hear Slobodan
Milosevic speak. The date of the speech was significant as it
marked the 600th anniversary of the 1389 Battle of Blackbirds in
Kosovo, the Serb people's most precious day.

The Serbs commemorate not only the location, but also the
battle, which is considered the founding of nationhood for the
Serbs, much in the way the Australians look to a defeat by the
Turks in Gallipoli in 1915 to define Australia's national character.

Not yet the President of Yugoslavia, nor even Serbia,
Milosevic was at that time trying to take control of the Serbian
Communist Party. While Milosevic gave his speech, he had plain
clothes policemen, dressed fraudulently as ethnic Albanians,
throw stones at the Serbian onlookers. This allowed Milosevic to
create a mood that the 'Serbs were under attack' and he,
Milosevic, proclaimed he would never allow Serbs to be beaten
again!

Milosevic created this false scenario to deliberately inspire
hatred and fear based on the national psyche of Kosovo being
home, but with it being under a false threat.

The Battle of Blackbirds was a great location for a political
manipulation as it was reminder of the long history of the Serbs
being ruled and repressed by Ottoman (Islamic) Turks seen as
synonymous in public culture with Albanian Muslims.

Milosevic deliberately created fear from a fabricated attack in
order to gain votes and support for himself. Unfortunately this is
not an unusual event in new democracies, or even some mature
ones.

It is a truism in politics that I was to learn many times over
during the coming years, that if given the choice between

preaching fear, hatred and intolerance on one hand, or togetherness, understanding and compassion on the other, the former wins almost every single time. The reason we look to leaders like Nelson Mandela as rare and gracious leaders is because they are exactly that, both rare and gracious.

There are many examples in history where a leader has deliberately and falsely created fear in order to gain votes. In Australia, for example, we could reflect upon the "child overboard" scenario around the time of the November 2001 Australian Federal Election.

In the lead up to the election the polling for the governing Liberal Party did not look good. However, following the terrorist attacks of September 11, 2001, Australia, like many countries, was fearful of terrorist attacks and vulnerable to manipulation of hatred of all things 'Muslim'.

In the early afternoon of 6 October 2001, a southbound wooden hulled "Suspected Illegal Entry Vessel" designated SIEV 4, carrying 223 asylum seekers and believed to be operated by people smugglers and carrying largely Islamic asylum seekers from Iraq and Afghanistan, was intercepted by the Australian Navy vessel HMAS Adelaide 100 nautical miles (190 km) north of Christmas Island (which is Australian territory) and then sunk. The next day, which was the day before the issue of writs for the 2001 federal election, Immigration Minister Philip Ruddock announced that passengers of SIEV 4 had threatened to throw children overboard in an effort to force the Australian Vessel to 'rescue' them and take them to Australia.

This claim was later repeated by other senior government ministers including Defence Minister Peter Reith and Prime Minister John Howard.

A later Australian Senate Select Committee found that no children had been at risk of being thrown overboard and that the government had known this prior to the election.

The government was criticised for misleading the public and cynically "(exploiting) voters' fears of a wave of illegal immigrants by demonising asylum-seekers". There are many people, me included, who believe that that fabrication was intentionally created to inspire hatred and fear of asylum seekers and thereby increase the votes for the Liberal Party in the 2001 election.

I see no moral distinction or differentiation between the actions of Milosevic at the Battlefield of Blackbirds and the actions of whoever fabricated the child overboard story.

I reinforce here that I do not suggest the Howard Government would go on to repeat the atrocities of Bosnia – clearly not - I restrict my comparison to Milosevic's political action of 1989. Both the Milosevic and Child Overboard scenarios deliberately created fear, falsely and deliberately, in order to gain political advantage.

I would like to have said that over the years Australia has changed. But even in 2012 we still see politicians doing the same thing. Australian Opposition Leader Tony Abbott still refers to asylum seekers coming by boat as 'illegal'.

Abbott knows this to be false.

On Tuesday 14 August 2012, ABC Melbourne Radio presenter Jon Faine pulled him up on this fact pointing out the Australian Migration Act 1958 allows for those seeking asylum to enter Australia, with or without visas. The same situation is covered by the United Nations Refugee Convention, of which Australia is a signatory. Whatever asylum seekers are, the one thing they are not is 'illegal'. Yet Abbott continued then and continues now to call them 'illegal', deliberately, falsely and knowingly.

So why would a person, knowing the use of a word to be false, still use it?

The only credible answer is the deliberate falsehood is used to inspire hatred and fear of asylum seekers in order to gain electoral advantage. Like in 2001 with John Howard's Child Overboard affair, I see no moral distinction or differentiation between the actions of Milosevic at The Battlefield of Blackbirds and the actions of Tony Abbott designed to deliberately create fear and falsehood to deliberately gain political advantage.

Carrots and Sticks can solve the debate.

Introduction

In 2011 I called for a change. I said that it was time to hit the reset button on the refugee debate, take a bipartisan approach to asylum, and resurrect Australia's brand image. In doing so I also set out a summary of how I believed Australia's asylum policy should be formed.

Multimedia (ebook only)

I spoke along similar lines to this article in a speech here.

The business community of Melbourne, deeply concerned about the brand image of Melbourne, Victoria and Australia, calls upon politicians of all sides to reconsider the debate on asylum and to create a mix of policy carrots and sticks to genuinely address the regional asylum problem.

Politicians from all sides enter the debate should hold with the best long term interests of Australia in mind, not their partisan short term interests.

I recently suggested a policy that offers the right mix of carrots and sticks, and suggested a framework for a regional negotiation that enhances Australia's reputation. It is a policy that does the following:

1. One, improves the conditions for asylum seekers – both those who arrive and those who are waiting in legitimate processing centres off-shore.

2. Two, satisfies the reasonable concerns around protection of Australian boarders.

3. Three, enhances not detracts from Australia's reputation.

Above all it improves seeks to move the debate from Ignorant and Fearful to Informed and Hopeful. It hopes to maximise Australia's opportunity to be the hinge, not the cringe.

Regional Asylum policy suggestion - Policy Philosophy:

Asylum policy must be designed to enhance not detract from Australia's reputation, and contain within it the carrots and sticks necessary for an orderly and humane treatment of asylum seekers.

Any policy must respect the sanctity of the Refugee Convention which is to provide protection from a well-founded fear of persecution, but not to be a de-facto mechanism for immigration.

The correct forum for the policy debate:

The asylum issue is a regional issue and therefore must be solved regionally. Currently the regional burden is being handled mainly by Malaysia and Indonesia. Malaysia currently has over 200,000 refugees, asylum seekers and 'persons of concern' listed by UNHCR, Australia has only 25,000. Australia needs to step up to the plate, take a fair share and need to do so from a regional perspective.

The Bali Process, and the Regional Cooperation Framework it created, is a good start to regionally discuss the plethora of complicated issues from trafficking, to law enforcement and durable solutions for asylum seekers. This forum could be used more to search for lasting solutions on resettlement and those resettlement issues should be the main focus of Australia's involvement, not location of processing.

The key driver of people smuggling:

Currently in Indonesia and Malaysia, once a refugee is assessed as genuine, and they pass through health and security checks, the still have to wait for many years for resettlement. If people have passed through health and security checks, and been assessed as a genuine refugee, why should they wait? This long wait causes a perception that there is no legitimate and genuine path to resettlement, hence people take the desperate act of getting on boats.

The deep flaw in the current asylum debate is that it is focussed on only one aspect: Processing. The location of processing – Australia, Malaysia or Nauru - is the wrong issue. The lack of rapid Refugee resettlement post processing in whatever location, not refugee processing itself, is the driver of the people smugglers trade. Speedy resettlement must therefore be the focus of regional response.

If there is a legitimate and speedy path to resettlement and stop the current long delays in resettlement post processing, we stop the market. If we stop the market, we stop the boats. If we stop the boats, we stop the deaths.

Policy Carrots and Sticks.

a.   Carrots.

Giving a realistic route to resettlement is the key to stopping the boats. Policy drivers must stop people hopping on boats in the first place. Turning boats around is too late.

The alternative path:

A regional treaty should be negotiated that would define an asylum seeker as 'arrived in the region' when they land in the county of first arrival by whatever means, land sea or boat – most often Malaysia or Indonesia. Each regional country should agree to bear a fixed percentage of the burden of refugees, with this burden including:

- a percentage of the cost share of processing
- a cost share of repatriation of non-genuine asylum seekers, and
- a fixed percentage of automatic acceptances and immediate resettlement of genuinely assessed refugees.

Asylum seekers would be assessed in country of first arrival with health and security checks undertaken as part of refugee assessment overseen by UNHCR in the country of arrival. If accepted as genuine refugees these people should be resettled immediately to whichever of the regional countries is under-quota on refugee acceptances with appropriate visas so allow work, education and genuine resettlement?

Refugees would not choose which country they are resettled in. They would be resettled in whichever country is next in line to accept refugees according to the resettlement percentages.

b.   Sticks

Should an asylum seeker elect not to use the path above, and still seek to come to Australia by boat, they would be processed on shore, but only be entitled to limited TPV style limited visas. This would act as a deterrent.

The balance of carrots and sticks.

A genuine regional solution like the above, if agreed, would take away the market for people smugglers as it would give a genuine alternative path to resettlement with the removal of the delay in resettlement. It would stop the boats.

If agreed the above policy would allow Australia to take a genuine regional approach and allow Australia to take its fair share of genuine refugees in a controlled, humane and dignified manner.

The policy would also remove the fear of terrorism as refugees would have been assessed for health and security.

This would not act as a 'pull factor' to Australia as refugees would be in a lottery for resettlement options, but would still be escaping the persecution that the refugee convention is designed to provide.

Resettlement is the key to asylum solutions

Introduction

Having worked for the UN High Commission for Refugees this article is one in a series I published from 2000 through to 2011 lamenting the great shame of the paucity of Australian public debate. Here is one offering solutions.

Multimedia (ebook only)
I spoke along similar lines to this article in a speech here.

The deep flaw in the government's asylum policies is that refugee *resettlement*, not refugee *processing* is the driver of the people smugglers trade. The location of processing is not relevant. The Gillard Government policy was flawed from birth and a replacement policy must recognise this fact.

If you want to break the people smugglers business model, as Chris Bowen says, then you must ensure rapid resettlement after asylum processing is complete, regardless of where that processing takes place.

Whatever policy follows on from the High Court's decision, it should have three objectives. One, improve the conditions for asylum seekers. Two, protect Australian boarders. Three, enhance Australia's reputation.

Each of the three major parties fails on at least one of these.

Arrival by sea has people embark on the dangerous journey those results in death for too many desperate people. Too many drown on route. The Greens are wrong to say 'let the boats land', not because we don't want refugees here, but because we don't want refugees to drown en route.

But the fear mongering coming out of the Coalition is also wrong. The Coalition policy is contributing to a negative brand image of Australia as an unwelcoming county. This must stop.

We receive such a small proportion of the global refugee intake. We are asked by some in the Coalition ranks "do we want those sorts of people here"? My response is to think: Do we want someone willing to risk their lives for nothing other than a better future for their children?

My answer: Absolutely we want that sort of person here. But we want them here in an orderly way.

Likewise the ALP's solution to ship people off to Timor, Malaysia or wherever they might think of next is misguided. It too does not discourage people from getting on the boats in the first place.

We need a refugee policy that reflects Australia's position as a leading country, not a fearful one. We should also balance the needs of the refugee and asylum seeker needs, as well as address the concerns of Australians around health and identity.

Giving a realistic alternative to boats as a route to resettlement is the key to stopping the boats. Turning boats around is too late. We need to stop them leaving by taking from the people smugglers their horrific trade. If we stop the delay in resettlement, we stop the market. If we stop the market, we stop the boats. If we stop the boats, we stop the deaths.

Currently in Indonesia and Malaysia, once a refugee is assessed as genuine, and they pass through health and security checks, the still have to wait for many years for resettlement.

If they have been processed as genuine and they have health and security checks, why make them wait?

Currently the regional burden is being handled mainly by Malaysia and Indonesia. Malaysia currently has over 200,000 refugees, asylum seekers and 'persons of concern' listed by UNHCR, Australia has only 25,000. Australia needs to step up to the plate, take a fair share and need to do so from a regional perspective.

A regional treaty should be negotiated that would define an asylum seeker as 'arrived in the region' when they land in the first county – most often Malaysia or Indonesia. Each regional country should agree to bear a fixed percentage of the burden of refugees, with this burden including a percentage of the cost share of processing and repatriation of non-genuine asylum seekers, and a fixed percentage of automatic acceptances and immediate resettlement of genuinely assessed refugees.

They should be processed in the country of first arrival with health and security checks are undertaken as part of refugee assessment overseen by UNHCR in the country of arrival. If accepted as genuine refugees these people should be resettled immediately to whichever of the regional countries that is under-quota on refugee acceptances.

Refugees would not choose which country they are resettled in. They would be resettled in whichever country is next in line to accept processed refugees according to the resettlement percentages.

This would discourage refugees coming with an aim to get to one particular country.

A genuine regional solution like the above would take away the market for people smugglers as it would remove the delay in resettlement. It would stop the boats. It would allow Australia to take a genuine regional approach and allow us to take our fair share of genuine refugees. Critically it would also remove the fear of terrorism as refugees would have been assessed for health and security.

It is time for a politician to stand up and lead. They should lead from the basis of both pragmatism and humanity, not just fear or populism.

Refugee health, our new stolen generation

Introduction

In October 2011, as more trends around refugee suicide and self-harm became clear, I release the following press release, based on my background as a former Head of Early Warning and Contingency Planning for the United Nations High Commission of Refugees and the son of a former Patrol Officer.

Refugee health, will be our new stolen generation. It is time to hit the reset button on the refugee debate, take a bipartisan approach to asylum, and resurrect Australia's image.

Tonight's Four Corners will show the lifetime devastation being caused to people in detention centres. We must stop the lifetime pain our national policy is causing, and it can be done if we start thinking about policy and not politics.

"Future generations will look back on our generation and ask 'why did you let that happen' just like we ask how previous generations let the Stolen generation happen", says former UN official and son of former patrol Officer, Andrew MacLeod.

"Politicians of all sides to reconsider the debate on asylum and to create a mix of policy carrots and sticks to genuinely address the regional asylum problem to avoid boats and detention", he says.

I have written to all parties and suggest a policy that offers the right mix of carrots and sticks, and suggests a framework for a regional negotiation that enhances Australia's reputation", says MacLeod.

It is a policy that does the following:

1. One, improves the conditions for asylum seekers – both those who arrive and those who are waiting in legitimate processing centres off-shore.
2. Two, satisfies the reasonable concerns around protection of Australian boarders.
3. Three, enhances not detracts from Australia's reputation.

"If we negotiate a regional solution aimed at rapid resettlement of refugees, then we wouldn't need Boats and wouldn't cause all this harm", he says.

In short MacLeod suggests a regional agreement that would define all asylum seekers as 'arrived in region' whenever they arrive in the first regional country by whatever method, land, sea or air.

A regional agreement would cost share the cost of processing based on a negotiated percentage, and then accept that same percentage of refugees for resettlement.

"Australia would take a fair share, as would Malaysia, Indonesia, Nauru, PNG, New Zealand and all regional countries.'

"We need to remember that the back of the people smuggler's business model is not location of processing, it is the lack of resettlement post processing" MacLeod says.

D: Gender and families

Feminism or Genderism; Which is the right way?

Introduction

While working for the UN and with Pakistani Army Generals in Pakistan I did a lot of learning, principally about gender planning, particularly after seeing programs that increased girls' enrolments in schools in Kashmir. After I saw that success and understood the need for age and gender desegregated data, and saw the issue not through the lens of feminism, but through the lens of effective planning I began to understand the "mainstreaming" of gender as an issue throughout all parts of the relief and recovery operations.

This is an extract from my upcoming book "Life Half Lived", to be published by New Holland Press in 2013.

One may be tempted to think an army general in a country like Pakistan would think the issues around gender would be secondary or inconsequential. Nadeem, the Vice Chief of General Staff, understood not only the importance of the issue and the importance of the planning but also the importance of persuading other men that gender issues are critical in project planning and implementation.

We both learnt that the issue around "gender" is not the same as issues about "women and girls". For example, many may look at the problems associated with female only households when all the men of a family have been killed in a natural disaster. Yet few think of the problems of male only households when all the women in the family have been killed. Regardless of what one may think of different cultures, when there are specific tasks in the family assigned to the different genders in different cultural environments, then a family unit becomes dysfunctional if one or other of the genders is removed from the equation. Those planning relief and recovery operations need to understand the various issues regarding gender and plan the response to those issues.

Both those who look at gender issues merely through a "feminist" lens and those who are straying down the path of male chauvinism, are equally as distracting as the other when it comes to planning a comprehensive response. Nadeem learnt this very quickly.

I was a little slower in learning. I attended an emergency planners' conference in Geneva during 2006 and listened to a presentation given by a gender advisor (the vast majority of whom are female) speak on issues regarding women's evidence in rape trials in Islamic countries. It is a great shame that in some Islamic countries women's evidence is not accepted as equal to that of a man's evidence.

At this conference the woman presenter outlined the programme she had been running in Sudan to have women's evidence accepted as equal to men's. She had persuaded approximately one hundred women who had been raped, and two had wished to put the episode behind them, to pursue a prosecution of the male perpetrators. This woman saw it as a great success that after one hundred attempts she achieved the first prosecution of a man based on the equal acceptance of women's evidence. The majority of the people in the room applauded her.

I put my hand up to ask what had happened to the other ninety-nine women. The presenter informed us that there had been no conviction in the previous ninety-nine cases and the men had walked free. I again asked the question about what happened to the other women as opposed to the accused men. After having admitted a sexual act took place in the course of a rape trial, but the man was found not guilty the women were then charged with adultery. They were convicted and stoned to death.

When one becomes too blinded to an ideological goal one can lose sight of their impact on people. Whilst this presenter thought it was a great success that after one hundred tries they received one conviction for rape, I thought it a great tragedy that ninety-nine women who had wanted to put the episode behind them ended up being charged with adultery, convicted and stoned to death. This would not have happened to them if not for the neo-academic feminist wanting to prove a point.

In a similar way, when gender issues are confused with feminism in issues regarding sexual and gender based violence in conflict environments, similar distortion can take place. Rape as a weapon of war is abhorrent. Yet if one looks at the issue of rape in war through a feminist lens then the result is the creation of a large number of programmes supporting the victims of rape. When one looks at the issue of rape as a weapon of war through a gender lens then two things become apparent. Firstly, it is appropriate to put in place as many programmes as you can to look after the victims of rape. Secondly, however, when looking through a gender lens and analysing who the perpetrators of rape are in many conflict environments, often it is young boys and youths forced into the acts as part of an initiation programme implemented by some of the world's worst warlords.

In many ways the boys who are kidnapped, forced into the military and forced to perpetrate these heinous crimes are also victims. When understanding this dynamic, a lot of programmes can be put in place to try and protect the boys from kidnapping and thereby reduce not only the number of child soldiers but also the number of perpetrators of the horrendous crime.

When looking through a feminist lens one deals with the consequence of rape. When looking through a gender lens one can deal with both the consequence of rape and the causes of rape. It is always best to stop the event from happening than to deal with the consequence afterwards. This is the difference between looking at issues from a "gender" as opposed to "feminist" perspective.

In the case of the Pakistan earthquake when looking through a "feminist" lens one may be tempted to say that girls were not going to school because of issues regarding Islam.

When looking at the issue through a "gender" lens one may see the issue has more to do with taps.

Parental leave or Maternity leave, which is it really?

Introduction

Before the last Federal election Australia was debating Paternity Leave options. I wrote the following Opinion Piece as part of the debate. This covers similar themes to my recent *genderism v feminism* piece in the last chapter.

I argued that we are so close to achieving the last great piece of social change and the conclusion of the fight of our mothers... and who was dumping the chance? The Minister for the Status of Women.

Born in 1966 I am one of the first so-called Generation X. I am part of the first generation of men who accept that women should an equal part of the work force. For men like me it is not debatable, equality just *is*.

Our mother's fought as feminists for the right to liberate women from the home and to give women the right to participate equally in the workforce. However one critical point was missed: True equality also requires the liberation of men from the workforce.

True equality requires equal opportunity for both genders to become the care-givers at home. True equality is for the liberation of men from the workforce as well as women from the home.

Therefore, somewhat ironically, the last great piece of social change from the feminist era is to liberate men. And in the last 48 hours we just blew it and women will bear the brunt.

There are three great hurdles as I see it to men becoming the primary care giver, one is financial, one biological and one cultural.

The biological issue is around breast feeding, an issue that I will not engage in here.

Financially in most relationships men, be it through gender or age (or a combination of the two) tend to earn more than women. Hence, a parental leave policy based on the minimum wage, such as that proposed by the government, will favour women being the primary care giver. A 'parental leave' policy based on minimum wage is merely a 'maternity' leave program with a nice name, not a genuine *parental* (i.e. maternity and paternity) leave program.

Such a program cements the role of females as care-givers, cements females in the role of having to take career breaks, and cements the women into a lower paid career path. After all, according to The Economist, it is not gender that creates the wage level gap in modern economies, it is parenthood.

According to The Economist, non-parent women get paid the same as non-parent men, but parent women get paid less than parent men. Parenthood and care-giving is the critical differentiation, not gender. Wage equality therefore depends in part on equality of care-giving as well as equality in the workforce.

On the other hand a parental leave program based on current wage levels earned, such as that proposed by the coalition, removes the financial disincentive for the male to be the primary care giver. Such a policy may encourage more men to be the care-givers and move towards an even more equal economy.

Surely equality is something that the left wing would agree with.

But now we get really bizarre.

The Coalition argues for a 26 week leave to be paid by the top end of town.

Excuse me? Top end of town? The Liberal Party?

Surely when the Liberal Party proposes a 26 week parental leave that further liberates women from the home and paid for by the top end of town, the left-wing-Emily's-List-females of the Labor Party would agree like Cheshire Cats with cream?

Surely the Labor Party, in pursuing the last great piece of social change, rather than reflexively opposing the opposition, would adapt the program and implement it with bi-partisan support?

"Yes Mr Abbot, good idea, let's work out the details and implement it this Parliament". Couldn't K Rudd and co. say that?

But no.

We now find ourselves in a strange situation. The government Minister for the Status of Women is arguing against a 26 week parental leave program that removes the financial disincentive for men to be care-givers, in favour of a program of 18 weeks that cements the women in the role of care givers.

You have the Labor Party arguing against a 26 week parental leave policy that many in the feminist movement have been calling for since I was a kid.

You have the Labor Party arguing against the top end of town paying for it.

I just don't get it. We are within distance of finishing the work of our mothers. We are within reach of genuinely looking at men and women being equal in the workforce *and* as care-givers.

We are so close to achieving the last great piece of social change... and who is dumping the chance? The Minister for the Status of Women.

Bizarre.

Do we need non-family as well as family policies?

Introduction
2011 census data showed a continuing trend of fewer people married, and more couples without children. Are Australia and Melbourne ready for this change? I wrote this in 2012 following the release of the data.

Consider this: According to the Department of Planning and Community Development, by 2025 up to 51% of Melbourne households will be 'no child households'. That is pre-child, post-child or no intention of having children.

We already see that the fastest growing segment of the housing market is the single person household, with predictions from DPCD of single person households reaching 44% by 2035.

This is a massive shift in our community that government and planners are not sufficiently alert to or ready for. We hear a lot from our political leaders about families, but if 51% of our population by 2025 will be living in a non-family set up, shouldn't we hear about non family policies as well?

Think through some of the ramifications in housing, social cohesion and fiscal policy.

Let's take housing. According to the Grattan Institute 84% of Melbourne's housing stock is made up of detached or semi-detached family homes. We can see a massive disconnect if by 2025 only 49% of our population will be in family units but 84% of the housing stock is aimed at them. There will be glut of family homes and a shortage of non-family medium and higher density living.

As the average number of people per household shrinks we will need more residences for the same amount of population. If we do not radically change the design of our residences then Melbourne will see a massive spread into greenfield areas causing a huge decrease in Melbourne's density.

Melbourne has seen a huge drop in its density from 20.3 people per hectare in 1960 to around 14.9 people per hectare today partly because the trend of shrinking family sizes has been going on since the 1960s. This decreasing density is eating up farmland on the urban fringe and putting huge strain on infrastructure spending as the cost per person per kilometre of infrastructure sky rockets.

This decreasing density caused by demographic change will continue even if the population remained exactly the same – let alone if we continue to grow our population at our 150 year average of 1.4% per annum.

If by 2035 this demographic change sees the predicted 44% of our population as single person households, imagine how catastrophic this problem will be if we do not build more higher-density single person dwellings? We must urgently start the change in our housing mix regardless of population growth, because even a stable population would see this trend.

Let's think also of some social issues that may arise from this trend.

As generation Y continue to grow and have a higher proportion of their human interaction through remote or virtual means such as Skype, Facebook and whatever social networks that will come next, will our society have a decreased ability to deal with each other face to face? In this age, how many of the residents of single person households will have little human interaction?

We know proportionally virtual interaction is rising at the expense of actual interaction. Some of this is good in maintaining international or interstate friendships, but how will this evolve in their future? How will it impact on our society and urban villages?

As single person households age and get ill, will we see more horror stories of people falling ill or dying at home and remaining undiscovered for days or weeks as 'friends' wonder why they have not been online?

I don't know the answers to these questions, but I do know that as a community we have not been 'asking' these questions enough. As our demography changes, how do we as a society meet the change?

Let's look at fiscal transfers. We have only just started to hear challenges to 'baby bonuses' family subsidies and the like. When will people start to ask, as they surely will, for 'non family' bonuses, payments or subsidies, or start to oppose family payments on the grounds that they are unjust?

Will we see arguments put that non family tax payers already subsidies family units enough through tax funded education which non families receive no direct benefit from?

Will non family units ask for additional age care support from government as they have no families to look after them in old age? Is there an argument that 'I paid for your child's education through my tax, now you pay for my age care through your tax'?

Again, I don't know the answer to these questions, but I do know that we must start asking these questions. 2011 was the first year that more baby-boomers left the job market than Gen Y entered the job market. It was the first year that our native workforce shrank and hence was the first year that the 'future ageing population problem' became the 'present aging population problem.

With decreasing family sizes, growing numbers of childless households and growing numbers of single person households, the enormous challenges of an aging and changing population are only just starting and we are just not discussing this enough.

About Gay Marriage.

Introduction
In 2013 further lobbying was undertaken for marriage equality. The lobbying prompted me to write the below.

Recently a number of people have put big white equals signs on their Facebook profile shots.

Just in case you are wondering what the big white equals sign means, it is for marriage equality.

Now, as a committed non-marriage guy, I really don't have a dog in this fight, other than to say:

Get over it. Change the law.

If people want to marry and make a public commitment to each other - let them. The state should not intervene and prevent people from voluntarily committing themselves to each other, and assuming the legal rights and responsibilities that such a commitment entails..

But nor should the state intervene and require religions to change their views and accept religious ceremonies for same sex couples.

So, a solution?

Let people be joined by recognised state officials (as mixed gender couples can today with celebrants or at the town hall). So let's define 'marriage' as a legal union between two people regardless of gender and get over that bit.

Let's then say that a 'holly union' or 'religious marriage', which will have no legal affect, is up to each religion to determine. A duly recognised religion can define requirements for members of its flock.

But this would require separating the legal act and the religious act. Is this a radical thought?

Perhaps it is in Australia or the US. But consider Europe.

In Switzerland for example, a couple must be legally married at the town hall for at least two weeks before any religious celebration.

So separating religious and legal 'marriage' is not such a big deal.

Best of both worlds if you ask me.

And if you are thinking of getting married, invite me and put me on the unattached table.

E: ECONOMIC AFFAIRS

Designed in Australia - built in the world. Have we missed out calling?

There is a lot of hand wringing and finger pointing regarding the collapse of Australia's car manufacturing business. But in all this finger pointing, is Australia missing a positive way forward?

Rather than cry over the spilt milk of a lost car industry, could Australia be a vital component manufacturing industry and a vibrant design hub instead? Could we perhaps expand our high end component manufacturing instead of trying to build entire cars? Have other advanced economies done this?

Switzerland has an economy that has a higher cost base than Australia and a currency that grew faster and stronger than the Australian Dollar since the GFC (with the Swiss Franc nearly 28% higher against the dollar than early 2008) - yet Swiss high quality, high end and high margin manufacturing industry not only thrives but grows.

Indeed according to the Swiss Chamber of Commerce and Industry, Industrial production is now more important to the Swiss economy than banking (see http://www.sccij.jp/news/overview/detail/article/2013/05/06/switzerland-manufacturing-bigger-than-banking/)

The survival of Swiss industry is based on a formula that has worked very well: build specialized products such as motors, turbines, and watches; guarantee the delivery date; offer the necessary financing through an efficient banking network; provide effective after-sales service; sell the product all over the world and thus achieve economies of scale.

Switzerland does not beat itself up about not having a Swiss made car brand (the Smart is a small niche and recent invention in partnership with German based Mercedes Benz). Instead the Swiss are happy that there is hardly a top end car in the world that does not have with in it Swiss made vital components.

Can Australia learn from Switzerland, a landlocked country, further from the booming Asian markets, more expensive than Australia but somehow thriving in manufacturing?

Could Australia do this? Did you know that for a long time most BMW wheels were made in Tasmania, back in the days when Tasmania led the world in niche alloy manufacturing and aluminium welding? But no, Australia did not celebrate the island state's success. Tassy only manufactured wheels, but Victoria made cars.

Australia should not let its component industry die. Rather lets support those components that are high end and high cost and support the creation and marketing into new territories. Like Switzerland, Australia could become a high quality producer, if only we focus on quality, flexibility and productivity.

What about design? When Mike Deveraux announced Holden's end to production, and politician after politician lined up to chastise him, did anyone ask him for his alternative view? When I was CEO of Committee for Melbourne I asked Deveraux for his long-term vision for Holden. He said to me "what is wrong with 'designed in Melbourne, built in the world'?".

Good question.

Deveraux outlined his vision for Holden Fisherman's Bend to be one of the three main design hubs for General Motors globally. It would have made Melbourne critical to GM around the world. Deveraux's vision was to work with authorities and redesign Fisherman's Bend in Melbourne to be a cool place to live and a cool place to work.

In many ways his vision was to take Fisherman's Bend 'back to the future'. The suburb was designed originally to be the dormitory suburb for those working in the factories there. As the suburb gentrified, the Holden workers were priced out and many ended up commuting daily from Dandenong. But the gentrification made the suburb cool and could attract the designers and artists necessary for a thriving design hub.

When in 2010 we at the Committee for Melbourne raised the prospect of re-developing Fisherman's Bend and took this idea to the Brumby and then Baillieu Governments. We received a good hearing. But when the redesign for Fisherman's Bend came out it specifically excluded areas occupied by Holden.

At CfM we organized for the Holden Government Affairs staff to meet Minister Guy's staff. We strongly supported the 'designed in Melbourne, built in the world' concept. It would give

Melbourne and Australia great relevance and a high employing industry.

But the government failed to listen and stuck to the government view didn't want to spook Holden away from manufacturing. Melbourne lost manufacturing and lost the opportunity to build a new suburb hand in hand with a global company that would have made it one of its three most important design hubs. An opportunity was lost.

Australian governments and Australian people have been so fixated on having an entire Australian car industry, that the country may have let slip the opportunity to be a vital part of a global industry in design and component manufacturing.

Australia should not fight the losing battle for an entire small cake, rather the country should fight for a good slice of a very big one instead. The country, so strongly against population growth, needs to recognize it choses to be a small domestic market. The only way its industry will survive is to be high quality, cost competitive and work much harder on niche marketing globally.

The Swiss have done it, why can't the Aussies?

Did the mining boom save Australia?

Introduction

It has almost become lore in Australia that the mining boom saved the country. It is almost as if the nation has to believe it is 'lucky' rather than celebrate some good planning. I included the following in a number of my speeches in 2010 and 2011.

Australians likes to say the country escaped the Global Financial Crisis because of the 'luck' of the mining boom and the mining sector.

This is too simplistic, but Australia prefers to say "lucky", rather than 'good management".

Why cannot Australia recognise that in escaping the global financial crisis Australia is seeing the culmination of three decades of very good policy across all political parties?

Factors impacting on our escapes from the GFC included:

- a combination of a flexible exchange rate (thanks to Hawke and Keating),
- a flexible labour market (thanks to Howard and Costello),
- the psychological impact of a well-timed (perhaps not well implemented) stimulus package,
- a strong and well regulated banking sector that has not collapsed (few in Australia would look to our four banks as saviours?) and,
- yes in part, the mining sector.

Whilst we are lucky with our resources, the other factors were a result of good planning.

Why doesn't Australia celebrate this? Is this the tall poppy syndrome again?

Why not rescue our largest export?

Introduction

During 2010, with a delicate international economy, I asked why is it that the perception Australians were creating of the country was neither accurate nor helping economically or socially. I used international education as an example.

Multimedia (ebook only)

I published this article in the Australian Financial Review and in The Melbourne Review *here* and spoke of these concepts during the Richard Searby oration, *here*.

Recent ABS statistics reveal a drop in population growth from 2.2% to 1.5%.

As natural increase has stayed relatively level, this drop is a result of a dive in net overseas migration - largely from international students. Whilst some may be relieved on the easing of pressure on our infrastructure, is this drop really a good or bad thing for Melbourne and Australia?

Education is Melbourne's second largest and formerly largest export. It is a larger export earner to Australia than gold, natural gas, wheat, and even beef. Education is so big that Access Economics equates it to around 1% of GDP; providing around 100,000 jobs to the economy, or about one job for every two higher education students in Australia.

Put another way, for every two international students lost, we lose one Australian job.

Curtin University's report 'The Economic Implications of Fewer Higher Education Students in Australia', showed international education was worth $10 billion to the broader Australian economy. Roughly 20% of the impact being in retail, 30% on accommodation and 33% on educational fees, with the remainder in day-to-day expenditure.

The fall in offshore applications for all education markets has seen a drop of nearly 23,000 students in 2011. That is 11,500 Australian jobs lost.

If the current drop is not cause for alarm, then the future projections out to 2015 should be. By 2015, some forecasts predict a drop of nearly 70,000 students against future expectations. If this comes true it would mean 35,000 fewer Australian jobs in the broader economy.

Alarmingly, 20% of these jobs would be in retail. That is 7,000 jobs in a sector in dire need of support.

So why are we not strongly fighting to protect this industry?

Rather than being concerned about jobs, for some reason our nation appears so fearful on population growth that we applaud the drop in arrivals without fully understanding the broader economic impact.

Perhaps we feel fluctuations in the dollar are the cause and are hard to control. This is only partially true.

Visa changes, while rightly reducing the poor quality education product, have also impacted on the high quality education product. By closing the door to the shonky operators, have we over-reacted?

An additional factor is more saddening.

Glenn Withers, the chief of Universities Australia said that the negativity surrounding Australian public debate on population, migration and refugees is "creating an impression that we are not welcoming students or even welcoming visitors."

These three factors are all coming together in, as a recent Deloitte Access Economics report says, in a perfect storm for the sector.

We must work urgently to alter the two that are in our control.

There is little at the macro level we can do on the dollar, we must work on the visa issues and we must reverse the negative brand image of Australia as unwelcoming.

As global uncertainty envelopes all industries, we must not see the education sector as an isolated victim, rather a strong indicator of threats to the broader economy.

It would be naive to think that negative perceptions of an unwelcoming are only affecting education.

Those involved in business, small, medium and large know that good reputation is critical to form successful business partnerships. When given a choice, people prefer to do business with people they like. It is human nature.

People, when given an alternative, may not want to do business with us, if we have created an impression that, to put it bluntly, they don't like.

If the education sector is the canary in the cage, and if the framing of national debate on population, refugees and immigration is portraying Australia as an 'unwelcoming' country, there is no doubt this will impact the broader economy and cost Australian jobs. If the estimation of 37,500 Australian jobs being lost by 2015 from the international education effect is true, how many more jobs will be lost in the broader economy if we do not reverse the image impact?

The perception of being unwelcoming derives from the views of some who say multiculturalism has not worked in Australia. They say that a reduction in migration would be a good thing.

Those who say such things are wrong.

We are a welcoming and well-functioning multicultural country and we must promote this image to protect our economy, most urgently in the education sector.

Australia has nearly half its population born overseas or with at least one parent born overseas. Whilst large proportions are from Europe, many are from Asia, South Asia, Africa and all over the world. Some of the oldest non-indigenous communities are the Afghanis and Chinese who arrived in the middle of the 18th century.

According to surveys we are the world's second most multicultural nation behind Luxemburg and equal with Switzerland – a land with four official languages and 22 Cantons.

Australia is ranked as the second most liveable country in the world, with Melbourne considered as the second most liveable city with less multiculturalism ALL ranking below us. Multiculturalism, albeit not perfect, has worked and is one of the great selling points for our economy.

So why do we allow an opposite impression to flourish and harm our reputation – and our business?

Part Three: The Future for Melbourne

A: POPULATION, PLANNING AND DEMOGRAPHICS

Getting better as we get bigger.

Introduction

In 2010-2011, Committee for Melbourne promoted a vision for Melbourne in 2060 that is even more liveable than 2010. To become more liveable CfM argued that the population needed to plan a city that would accommodate its population in a better way than even then.

In 2010 in my role of CEO of the Committee, I published the following, intended to lift the level of debate in the city.

It is important to note that the figure should be based on a realistic figure - neither unachievably high nor unachievably low. If we extrapolate the 150 year growth average for Melbourne for a further 50 years we would get a realistic 'continuity figure - i.e. continuing for the next 50 years that which we have done for the last 150.

If we continue out 150 year average of 1.4% per annum, not the spike of 2.2% we saw 3 years ago, we wouldn't get to 8 million until 2060. This is not a figure that CfM 'aims' for, rather a figure that logical analysis says is likely.

Even if you take the anti-growth views of people like Kelvin Thomson into account we would still reach that figure. Thomson, who argues for population controls on migration and financial disincentives from government for people to choose their family sizes, would see Melbourne reach 8 million by 2096.

On the growth figures that Melbourne experienced in 2008 of 2.2%, the city would reach 8 million by 2042.

Committee for Melbourne plots a moderate middle course of 2060, based on the 150 year growth average (Melbourne grew at an average rate of 1.4% for the past 150 years).

Some people are scared by this number. But regardless of whether it is 2096, 2060, or 2042, unless Melbourne becomes ugly or an economic wasteland, 8 million will be reached at some point in the future. Recent discussions have become bogged down in a debate about numbers. The best debate is not about numbers or time frames. The debate is about the Vision. The question then is how do we plan for it?

Many issues will need to be planned and resolved if Melbourne at eight million is to maintain its status as one of the World's Most Liveable Cities. We will need a vision for our future, much as Hoddle had a vision when he planned the CBD grid. Our vision will need to be equally as broad ranged as Hoddle's.

One of the many questions that we face in visioning Melbourne is: Where will all these people live? Will we have many more Docklands? Will we see Fisherman's Bend as a new residential heartland?

Many people have a view on Docklands, some positive and some negative, but does the Docklands development provide us some lessons in determining *how* we plan, and *where* we plan, future growth?

Take Fisherman's Bend for example. Surely we could extend Docklands all through there?

Fisherman's Bend, the area separating the south bank of the Yarra from Port Melbourne is, when looking only at the map, ideally placed for residential development. Tell me Web Dock would not be a great place to live, surrounded on three sides by water?

Currently it is a giant car park.

Closer to the CBD than St. Kilda, potentially more accessible than Footscray, surrounded by great suburban locations, yet Fisherman's Bend is made up of light industrial lands.

There are reasons for this. Some industries went in back in the days when Fisherman's Bend was to be Melbourne's airport. Some industry is there to service the Port. Some industry is there as the Garden City area of Port Melbourne, where I did a paper round as a kid, was envisaged as a cheap dormitory area for the industrial workers.

Now the prices have gone up and many of those working in Fisherman's Bend have long commutes.

The vision of close housing and work no longer applies, due to changes in area based demographics.

However, major decisions need to be made before Fisherman's Bend could be a great new Docklands.

182

Where would the Industry such as Holden go? How could we cost effectively move the different industries and employers without risking jobs and production? How would we clean up the contaminated land and who would pay for it? Where would you put the Port?

Clearly, if we take a short and a medium term vision, say five to 20 years, the cost effectiveness of a conversion of Fisherman's Bend would not stack up. We would leave it as an industrial area and try to find other interim solutions for a growing population.

But what of the longer term vision? What of Melbourne at eight million?

When planning a major city, or the significant growth of a major city, a long term comprehensive vision is surely more likely to lead to a better city, than short term ad-hoc responses, or medium term incremental changes.

We do not argue that Fisherman's Bend could provide the entire solution, or only solution, to a growing Melbourne. Nor does the Committee for Melbourne put forward the view that Fisherman's Bend *must* become residential.

My point is more subtle than that. My point is that many other growth options open up, many other solutions can be found, when a long term visionary approach is taken to planning Melbourne. Short and medium term plans don't give us exciting options for moving forward, geographically, economically, culturally and socially.

In a series of Shaping Melbourne Reports, Committee for Melbourne has engaged the community to look more at Density, Infrastructure, Community and Governance and will ask us all to look at the vision.

Above all our series of reports will call upon all of us Melbournians to engage in that 'Vision thing'. If we get the vision right, we get the city right. If we don't get the vision right then we get whatever just happens to come to pass.

Decreasing Density is Dangerous

Introduction

In 2011 I spoke at the Growth Areas Authority on density and the challenge Melbourne faces if we do not stop our decreasing density.

Multimedia (ebook only)

My short presentation is here. An edited version of this article was published in the Herald Sun on 30 October 2011, here.

Far from the perception that Melbourne's skyline is 'Manhattanising', Melbourne's density has nearly halved over the last fifty years. Melbourne's density decreased from 20.3 people per hectare in 1961 to 13.7 people per hectare in 1996. By 2001 Melbourne had recovered slightly to 14.5 and now around 15 people per hectare. Decreasing density is economically, socially and environmentally unsustainable. It must stop.

Our decreasing density has occurred because the average footprint of our houses is growing, and the average number of people in our houses is shrinking. Rather than growing upwards, our city keeps growing outwards. It is eating up greenfield land on the fringe.

This spread is increasing road congestion too.

While some people think inner city density is increasing road congestion, the truth is the opposite. Inner city people have the option of public transport. Outer city people don't. It is often the outer city residents driving in to the city that increases the congestion once they reach the middle or inner ring suburbs.

I am not blaming the outer suburbs people for this. They have to use cars when there is no public transport. And part of the reason is that public transport is much more expensive per person-kilometre in low density areas. Our population doesn't allow increased taxation or national debt to allow the government to build it.

This is why ultra-low decreasing density is so dangerous. It is more expensive to put in infrastructure in low density areas and more people drive. Bad economically, bad environmentally.

Sensible density is better – like the density levels we used to have. Melbourne could accommodate the predicted 6 million by 2035 people with the same density that Melbourne had before we started the mad rush to decreasing density.

Our current public discussion is dominated by the 'Planning Backlash' group, who is robbing from people the choice to live in medium or higher densities if they so choose, by objecting to any and all development and telling us to limit our population size, implying a limitation on people to choose their family size.

Our housing mix must have within it a range of housing option so all our citizens can have a choice of how they live, not just be forced into stereo typical one size fits all family homes.

I am not saying family homes are bad. Family homes are good for families. But by 2025, 51% of households in Melbourne will be no child households. That is pre-child, post child or no child.

While 51% of our households will be no child households, according to the Grattan Institute, 84% of our housing stock is family homes.

We have enough family homes in Melbourne for families; we do not have enough non family homes for people who prefer to live in less low densities.

Decreasing density is Still Dangerous.

Introduction
Those against housing development ignore one critical point.
People like to breed and therefore our population grows. Unless they
can find a way of slowing population, we must plan for a growing city, as
that is what will happen. Failure to plan leads to congestion and
pollution. With my earlier calls still unheeded, I repeated the argument.

Multimedia (ebook only)
An edited version of the following article appeared in The Age,
Thursday 14 June 2012, here.

For over two years I led Committee for Melbourne. During that time the Committee pushed had to improve dialogue and community discussion on density and urban planning. Given that the greater Melbourne area density dropped from 20.3 people per hectare in 1960, to near 13 by 1999, the Committee spoke strongly against the decreasing density of Melbourne.

Decreasing density is dangerous as it makes infrastructure like roads, public transport, gutters, power lines and all sorts of services much more expensive per person per kilometre. What is more, outer urban spread not only eats up valuable farm land, outer urban spread increases inner urban congestion. It does so as the outer suburbs are poorly served by public transport, forcing more people into cars that converge in the inner urban suburbs.

Decreasing density was seen by the Committee as one of Melbourne's greatest threats, and now we see the urban growth boundary extended again, decreasing our density again.

During my time at Committee for Melbourne, some accused the Committee, and me as CEO, as simply being the mouthpiece of developers. Now that I am free from the Committee what are my views now?

Over the last few months I have spent significant time in two vastly different cities that take a differing approach to density and public transport: London and Salt Lake City.

London is a low rise city. It has an urban density over three times that of Melbourne, but without sky-scrapers. It does so by having consistent four story (or there about) development across the entire city. Those who object to the 'Manhattanisation' of the CBD and Docklands may like the concept.

The fairly consistent level of higher density across the city is one of the reasons that public transport is less of an impact on the public purse and, at least within the M25, provides much better access to most of the city than automobiles.

On the downside, thin roads and four story heights along most streets restrict the amount of light that gets to the ground, adding to a 'compressed feel' in many parts of the city. I don't like the consistent feel of 'compression', although that is a subjective opinion. There are pros and cons to the 'London option' of medium to density everywhere.

Salt Lake City in Utah has a population of around 900,000 and an average density almost equal to Melbourne's, but very little public transport. With much higher automobile usage, little public transport and a particular weather related inversion affect in winter, Salt Lake City suffers from days of poor air quality. Public transport provision may help clean the air, but the retro-fitting of public transport into low density areas though is extremely expensive.

With low density, cycling is less of an option with a need to cover greater distances. With poor public transport provision, at least in comparison to London and Melbourne, the residents of Salt Lake City have little choice but to use cars. As fuel prices become more expensive there will be community impacts as well as the environmental impacts of so many cars.

So what lessons can we take for Melbourne?

Firstly, quality of life is improved with good public transport provision. Secondly, retrofitting public transport into low density cities is extremely expensive. It is far better to build public transport as one builds a city. Even in London the outer urban areas are less well served by public transport and retrofitting is tough. Thirdly, while there can be too much density like Mumbai, there can also be too little density as in our very own outer suburbs.

So why is Melbourne allowing the government to extend the urban growth boundary rather than looking for better urban density designs? Is it because we fear the voices of the anti-development set? And if we do opt to extend the city, why are we doing so without provision of decent public transport – particularly rail based light rail, trains and trams – to these new areas?

In effect Melbourne is becoming a city of numerous types. Outer urban Melbourne is becoming like Slat Lake – ultra low densities and poor public transport provision. The cost of this is not felt just by those living on the urban fringe. Food prices for all may go up as market gardens get gobble up. Air quality - as more car journeys take place in the outer urban areas - impact on everybody. Inner urban congestion increases if more people live in the outer urban areas without public transport options.

So should we go the London option – 4-5 stories everywhere?

In my subjective opinion – and it is subjective – is that variety is better. Areas of high density in areas like the CBD, Docklands and Fisherman's Bend makes sense and provide high density options for people who prefer that option. As do areas of higher density around activity centres.

Four story medium density design around public transport nodes also make sense, and provide options for people who prefer to live in that type of housing. Likewise having suburban streets with lower density makes sense to give people those living options – provided that public transport and service provision is available. Transport and services are available in established suburbs, we must demand provision in outer suburbs too. We must be prepared to pay for the provision as well.

The one thing we should not do, is extend the urban boundary which may give a perception of doing 'something', but without thinking of the proper balance for the city, the proper provision of public transport and services and without realising that the danger in doing so impacts on all residents of Melbourne.

Rather than taking the hard solution to consult with the community and determine where out density mixes are going, we are again simply extending our boundary and again falling into the trap of decreasing density. Strangely enough, when freed up from the Committee for Melbourne, and being free to express my own view, I find myself saying the same thing - decreasing density is dangerous.

A great city is a planned city

Introduction

As part of the on-going Melbourne Beyond Five Million series, I published this article outlining the future of the city. Melbourne in 2010 was the world's second most liveable city, climbing to number one in 2011.

Multimedia (ebook only)

I spoke along similar lines at the Growth Areas authority, *here*.

Melbourne is a feast for the senses. From our glorious architecture reminiscent of years gone by, to our contemporary cafe lifestyle; from our scenic open spaces, to our eclectic mix of world culture - yes, we Melbournians are a lucky bunch.

It's no surprise Melbourne is the world's second most liveable city; and our liveability cannot be taken for granted. In 1990, Melbourne took out top honours in the World's Most Liveable City ranking. Since then, we have fallen to number two. By comparison, Detroit was ranked six in 1990. Today, it's ranked 40 and falling fast.

As we get bigger, we cannot let our liveability slip through our fingers. We are obligated to not only maintain our city's liveability, but enhance it for years to come. Quite simply, it is up to us to build Melbourne's future.

For over 25 years, Committee for Melbourne has helped shape Melbourne's economic, social and environmental outlook. Founded in 1985 by a group of thought leaders who perceived a threat to Melbourne's reputation, the Committee continues to play a key role in positioning Melbourne as one of the world's most liveable cities.

Committee for Melbourne is a not-for-profit, apolitical, member network that unites Melbourne's finest leaders and organisations to ensure that that city's economic, social and environmental fabrics remain inclusive, progressive and sustainable.

Members represent over 150 of Melbourne's major companies, academic institutions and civic organisations who debate key issues affecting Melbourne's appeal. Through their expertise, leadership, insight and passion, members have supported some of our city's best initiatives including:

- The concept behind Melbourne's Docklands
- The introduction of the free City Circle tram
- The installation of bud lighting in Collins Street and St Kilda Road
- The development of the infrastructure bonds that funded CityLink
- The push for privatisation of Melbourne airport with direct flights into Melbourne

Today, the Committee is working to address issues that are set to impact Melbourne's liveability over the next 50 years. Our city can get better as it gets bigger, but only if we have a long-term plan ready.

This plan must address a number of things. Firstly, it must consider ways to build upon existing infrastructure to improve Melbourne's transport network.

Melbourne is approaching a system wide, city wide, mobility crisis caused by kevel crossings.

The Committee has identified rail level crossings as the hinge point issue preventing more trains operating on our city's rail system. With more Melbournians using the rail network each year level crossings will stay closed and the roads will clog up. Melbourne's 172 level crossings - Sydney has 8 - are the hinge point issue. At 100 million a pop, 17.2 billion needs to be found. Investing in rail and road separation will be vital to ease Melbourne's road congestion long-term. Committee members are working together to explore ways to remove Melbourne's most troubled level crossings in ways that are economically, socially, environmentally viable.

Secondly, the plan should also incorporate options for a good housing mix (i.e. low, medium and high density design). The Grattan Institute's recent *The Housing We Choose* report reveals that Melbourne is not building the types of houses people want or can afford. In fact, most people would consider the size and price of a property as trade-offs, if that property was in a good location. Put simply, with 51% of households being no child households by 2025, the great Australian dream is changing.

Therefore, we must integrate housing options in our communities to remain socially cohesive long-term. But for community to embrace different housing options, they first need to understand them. Committee members are working to identify the lessons learnt from Melbourne's Docklands to apply to the redevelopment of urban renewal areas such as Fisherman's Bend.

Thirdly, a plan for Melbourne should also actively protect our city's international image, particularly when it concerns Melbourne's second largest export – higher education.

To position Melbourne as a first-choice education destination within the international marketplace, we must improve the international student experience. The Committee's successful Culture Card program provides international students with positive cultural experiences to enhance their understanding and deepen their connection with Melbourne and Victoria. Now in its second year, the Committee continues to help international students settle in our city.

But, our international reputation doesn't end with international students. The Committee has also helped form a global secretariat on corporate social responsibility by supporting the new Melbourne-based UN Secretariat for Social Investment.

Finally, our long-term plan must nurture the future leaders of our great city. Operating since 1996, the Committee's business leadership program, Future Focus Group, develops the skills of our emerging leaders by encouraging them to develop and implement projects that make a tangible, positive difference to Melbourne. The Committee continues to provide our city's future leaders with the training needed to direct Melbourne's future.

It's true. A great city is a planned city, and Melbourne can get better as is gets bigger. But, we must plan now. If we fail to, we may become Detroit.

Melbourne needs a 50 year plan.

Introduction

In 2011 the new Premier Ted Baillieu had been in office for around a year. That was enough time to settle in. 2012, I said, had to be the year of delivery. The views were covered in the local media and largely recovered points raised over the previous two years.

Melbourne was elected the World's Most Liveable City in 2011. In 2012, we must strive to maintain and enhance our liveability. Whilst 2011 saw many reviews by the new State Government, 2012 must be the year of delivery and vision, not just analysis. 2012 must protect and enhance Melbourne's liveability. Planning for greater urban Melbourne will be the biggest delivery challenge.

Melbourne prides itself on being a well-planned city. But as we continue to bask in our city's number-one-ranking-glory, threats creep up on Melbourne's horizon. If we don't act now, Melbourne's liveability will slip through our fingers.

Committee for Melbourne has called for the Victorian State Government to invest in a visionary 50 year plan for Melbourne. The Government's promised Metropolitan Planning Strategy (MPS) should be delivered soon. It must set the needed vision for a greater-urban Melbourne. The MPS must allow the community to debate, discuss and agree upon a vision for Melbourne. The MPS must set the trend for the housing, infrastructure, transport and community services needed to support Melbourne's growth over the next 50 years.

Our challenge will be to shape Melbourne's future in the face of population and demographic change. This means we will need to think long-term and build what our children and grandchildren will need.

By 2025, 51 per cent of households in Melbourne will be no-child households, yet 84 per cent of our housing stock is made up of family homes. The MPS should give us guidance on how we can change our housing mix overtime.

With the single person household being the fastest growing component of our population, we need to ensure the future city is designed for more single person dwellings and services, as well as family dwellings and services.

Over the last 50 years, Melbourne's density has decreased to dangerously low levels. MPS must address this. According to the Department of Planning and Community Development, Melbourne's density decreased from 20.3 people per hectare in 1961 to 13.7 people per hectare in 1996. By 2001 we had recovered slightly to 14.5 and now around 15 people per hectare. Decreasing density is economically, socially and environmentally unsustainable. It must stop.

Committee for Melbourne believes that to help prevent this decrease in density, government must fix the urban growth boundary. Its continual expansion is economically, socially and environmentally unsustainable. New housing estates in new suburbs need roads, schools, parks and community services – this is a very expensive way to tackle population growth. Our way of thinking needs to get smarter.

Late last year, the Baillieu Government's $200 billion draft Growth Corridor Plan failed to consider balance between new developments with existing suburb revamps to tackle population growth. The Committee would like to see the MPS consider ways to enhance existing suburbs by including a greater mix of housing options and using infrastructure that's already in place.

The MPS should also set a goal for enhanced public transport usage, lower greenhouse emissions and continue to slow and then reverse the decreasing density of Melbourne. Committee for Melbourne believes that for the MPS to be effective, it must consider better infrastructure financing and coordination and align this with more intelligent land use planning.

Melbourne is facing a city wide, system wide, mobility crisis point because of the city's rail level crossings. With patronage growing by an estimated 5 per cent per year, increased train services will be needed to cater for this demand. Booms gates are already causing major delays on Melbourne's roads, and if train services increase, this will throw Melbourne's road traffic into chaos.

So far, Melbourne has been slow to remove its rail level crossings. Two separations were completed during the former Kennett government and two during the former Bracks/Brumby governments respectively.

Committee for Melbourne believes government needs to get serious about removing Melbourne's rail level crossings. It has committed to remove 10 during its first term. It's a start, but with over 170 level crossings throughout Melbourne, much more is needed. Alliances between the private and public sector could form part of the solution in funding this $17.2 billion problem, and the Committee is exploring ways to enable this to happen.

Above all, State Government must continue to resist the calls of a loud, but small minority, who call for limiting population growth. Sydney is a great example of what happens if government plans for a limited population growth. Twelve years ago, Bob Carr caved in to the 'anti population' lobby and said 'Sydney is full'. This had no effect on the growing population, but meant there was inadequate investment in infrastructure which resulted in a decline in Sydney's liveability and competitiveness as a global city. We must not allow Melbourne to repeat this mistake.

Seventeen Billion? Can we afford not to?

Introduction

In early 2011 Federal Liberal MP Greg Hunt spoke to Committee for Melbourne and called for a new type of bi-partisanship and a new type of community consultation. It is precisely that sort of consultation that is needed to solve Melbourne's $17 Billion level crossing problem. I agreed with Greg and followed up with the article: 'Is it time for bipartisan liberalism?' earlier in this book.

Federal Liberal MP Greg Hunt spoke to Committee for Melbourne and called for a new type of bi-partisanship and a new type of community consultation.

"In Australia we look at bi-partisanship and community consultation in a superficial way", he said. "We present our plan and demand people come on board."

It is time to heed that call. The community must be empowered to engage in a genuine decision based consultation - a consultation that addresses the compromises we face in order to tackle the challenges associated with Melbourne's growth.

Of the many challenges we face, and perhaps the most widespread, is the little understood $17.2 billion transport challenge posed by level crossings.

The separation of road and rail does not at first seem like a critical issue – but it is. In fact it could be considered one of the hinge point issue for Melbourne's transport infrastructure.

Level crossings are one of the single biggest restricting factors in increasing train frequency in Melbourne.

Currently there are 172 level crossings within Melbourne's Urban Growth Boundary. Sydney, by comparison has only 8.

And this is the problem: If you put more trains on the network then the boom gates are down longer and the roads clog up.

This creates a series of problems for Melbourne's community as safety becomes jeopardised by frustrated motorist avoiding boom gate closure, and the cost of congestion being forecast to rise from $3 billion per year to $6.1 billion by 2020.

If that is the financial cost, what about the practical?

Most public transport experts will tell you that for public transport to be truly effective service need to be so frequent the time table doesn't matter. Studies show this to be a service of eight minutes or more frequent.

That would mean on any given single line level crossing, a train would pass one way or the other every four minutes – and with a total closure time of two minutes that means every level crossing would be closed two out of every four minutes on single line crossings. On multiple line level crossings it would be more often.

Indeed if you were to put enough trains on the Dandenong line to meet current demand – not future demand – then the level crossings along the Dandenong line would be closed for almost the entire morning and evening peak period.

One doesn't need to be a town planner to realise that such a disruption to traffic flow would create road chaos. So if the problem is evident why can't the government fix it? The answer is cost.

At an average of around $100 million per level crossing the total bill would be $17.2 billion and government simply cannot afford it.

My question is, can Melbourne afford not to?

Our current rail network capacity is overloaded by roughly 40 per cent, and increasing. If we want more trains at increased frequency we have to accept that the roads clog up from level crossing closures, or we pay to upgrade the infrastructure.

Only two grade separations were completed by the Kennett government and two during the Bracks/Brumby government terms.

Currently the Baillieu government has committed to 10 in the first term, which is better than the predecessors. But at that rate it would take us 17 terms - or 68 years - to clear Melbourne's level crossings.

If we chose to pay, either we fund them through government debt and taxation and accept the slow delivery program, or we look to offset the infrastructure costs by allowing mixed-use development over viable level crossing sites.

We all know that any form of commercial development around train stations and level crossings is likely to ignite NIMBYism, led by well-meaning but small focussed groups. But we need to accept at a broader community level that change is required to improve our greater metropolitan liveability.

There are many tough calls to make, and genuine trade-offs to consider. The community must be consulted during these decisions.

The private sector is part of our community, and we see an opportunity for solution driven discussions to be focused on alleviating the problems of Melbourne's most troubled level crossings.

The Committee for Melbourne would like to begin exploring ways which the private sector could help offset the economic, environmental and social costs of separating road and rail. Our members have indicated to us there is an opportunity for business to assist in delivering some of this critical infrastructure if the community and planning frameworks are supportive.

We would like to see the birth of Greg Hunt's vision for a new community engagement where business, community and government come together to discuss problems together with a focus on delivering solutions – not just plans and proposals.

We cannot afford to continue sort term and shallow policy debate. We cannot afford to continue a slow fix on issues like Grade Separation.

Issues like grade separation can be used to reignite longer term thinking and better policy across a broad range of areas and re-engage democracy. We have been lacking long term thinking and planning for some time. We need to bring it back.

Melbourne's great architecture

Introduction

I gave the following speech to the Institute of Architects in Melbourne in 2010 with it appearing in their annual publication.

Melbourne is a city of some great architectural juxtaposition. Old and new. Think Museum and Exhibition Centre. Or Rialto.

Melbourne has, in its past, had some architectural horror stories, but Gas and Fuel thankfully left the scene.

Over the last twenty years, the architecture of modern Melbourne has developed to the extent that it is a great city, staying connected to its past and looking forward to its future.

Having recently returned from many years abroad I am now in the great position of coming home and being an expatriate at the same time. This experience has allowed me to wander the streets with the awe of a tourist and also the sense of belonging and being at home.

Now Melbourne is a handsome city. Down the road from what is without doubt one of the most beautiful major cities in the world, Melbourne has no great harbour and bridge, instead built architecture is what makes Melbourne handsome.

So what of the future?

The Committee for Melbourne is a 100% private sector funded organisation committed to improving the future of Melbourne. It is made up of Melbourne's leading 170 organisations and businesses, including many of the top architectural firms, who come together to do networking, activities and policy advice to government to keep Melbourne amongst the world's most liveable cities.

The Committee for Melbourne is focussing the energies and enthusiasm of its members on Melbourne's future as the greater urban area grows in population and perhaps size. The input of the member architectural firms in this thinking is critical.

We believe that the current debate on population size misses one critical point: Melbourne will get bigger and it can get better as it gets bigger.

Think about this: Melbourne in 2010 is twice the size of Melbourne 1960. At four million instead of two, Melbourne is unambiguously better in 2010 with twice the population, than it was in 1960 with half.

We therefore have already proved that you can get bigger as you get better. Our parents did it.

Can this continue? If we have become better as we got bigger while doubling from 2 million to 4 million, can we also get better as we double from 4 million to 8 million sometime in the second half of the century?

The Committee for Melbourne believes we can get bigger and better, but only if we plan it. Melbourne will not accidentally get better; it has to be thought out.

Is Docklands that bad?

Introduction

After a decade away, I found Melbourne's new but much maligned Docklands to be an alien in Melbourne. It still has challenges to adapt, and challenges in perception. It is an architectural 'new Australian' as I argued when this was first published.

Multimedia (ebook only)

This article was first published in The Sydney Morning Herald here and also in The Age, both in March in 2010.

When I left Melbourne some years ago Docklands was an idea not a reality. Back then urban living was a new idea being tested in Melbourne. Familiar in other higher density cities, apartment living in Melbourne was not the norm.

Back then I wondered how docklands would fit into 'Melbourne the city of villages'. Would it work or would the elephant remain a glorious white?

Now that I have returned home to Melbourne I have set out to test Docklands by taking an apartment. I want to know if the apartment lifestyle fits in Melbourne's city of villages and given our city of villages, would I *want* an apartment lifestyle.

So what is the verdict?

The first thing to note is the absence of children.

Most Melbournians do not bring families up in apartment blocks. There are some public housing exceptions, and exceptions in some inner urban areas in small art-deco style blocks like one I spent some of my school years in. However, generally, Melbournians aspire to a house with at least some garden when they think to have children.

Given the price range of apartments in docklands, starting from a minimum of $500,000 or more for a small two bedroom place, those that can afford Docklands as a destination would also have several suburban housing options within the same price bracket.

The result – an absence of children. Perhaps this is why there is no school in Docklands.

So who would live in Docklands given Melbourne's culture?

The answer seems to be visitors and students, temporary contractors, some empty nesters and some committed Dual-Income-No-Kids (DINKIES). None that I have spoken to perceive Docklands to be their lifetime habitation. Docklands is no Hawthorn, Albert Park, Craigieburn or others.

Is this a bad thing?

Expecting Docklands to be a 'community' or village like other areas of Melbourne seems to me to be unreasonable due to the demographics. Holding it to the standard of our village suburbs therefore is not fair.

That docklands is not a village, in the Melbourne sense, is not necessarily a bad thing. As our city grows and global workforces become more mobile, and as jobs become more temporary, having an urban area designed for this fluid market is not a bad thing – it is just a different thing.

This leads me to the second issue of accessibility. Many people have told me that there is an accessibility problem with the docklands. I am struggling to see why they say this.

Where I live in docklands is five minutes' walk from the Clarendon Street shops. There are CBD trams services in the heart of Docklands, and there is a direct tram link to the MCG. So why don't people see it as accessible as it is?

Perhaps it is because we perceive Docklands in an east-west sense alone, not a north-south sense.

For me an after work walk and drink takes me south, over the footbridges and onto South Melbourne and up Clarendon Street. My view of Docklands is not just up into the CBD it is to the south as well.

Perhaps what Docklands has is a *perception* of access problem, not the *reality* of access problem. Perhaps many people see Flinders Street as a city loop connection, but forget Southern Cross Station.

Spencer Street seems to be a mental border, and potential integration into southern suburbs, and possibly one day into Footscray, has not been well enough made.

So while we may accept the demographics of Docklands as new, and can work on the accessibility issues, a third issue raises its head.

Surprisingly to me Docklands is windy – very windy. I don't know why this is the case and one day I will button hole a weatherman in an elevator and ask. But the problem is not why it is windy; the problem is that it just IS.

How can we make a promenade area work, with outdoor cafes and pleasant walks, when the wind threatens to cool your coffee too fast, blow your napkin into your food and make conversation difficult? This will be an architectural challenge as, absent climate change, I don't know how we can make the wind go away.

Docklands is no village, but that is not a bad thing. It is incredibly easy to live in, it makes access to a CBD workplace simple, it is but a short walk from many major attractions and it is one of the few places in Melbourne where you could live without owning a car.

It has accessibility issues and its windy nature is a challenge, yet, in a large city Docklands will service a segment of the population well.

In the end Docklands is different to the rest of Melbourne. However, rather than seeing it as a black sheep, or see it as the new kid in school we should pick on, let's see it as the new comer to our culture for us to welcome and learn about. It is an architectural 'new Australian'.

Let's explore its difference and absorb what it has to offer. Like the new cultures and nationalities making a home in Melbourne, Docklands is like a new ethnic group that is now part of Melbourne. Explore it and embrace it, but don't expect it to be something it can't.

After Docklands, where next? What is the next big 'Vision'?

Introduction

While CEO of Committee for Melbourne, we promoted the view that Fisherman's Bend district of Melbourne should become a new residential area. The following article was first published in The Age in 2010, with a change in Government Policy along the lines outlined soon following.

In recent debates many people have argued that Melbourne will have a larger population. These discussions have become bogged down in a debate about numbers. The truth is that the number isn't the debate nor is the time frame. The debate is about the Vision.

The Committee for Melbourne believes that one day Melbourne will have eight million inhabitants and that Melbourne could be a better place, or a worse place, as a result of the growth - depending on how well that increased population is planned.

We estimate that the eight million mark will be passed around 2060, as 50 years ago our population was around half that of now, and fifty years from now it should be around double. Changes in population policy may bring the date forward a bit, or set it back a bit so arguing an exact date is fruitless. Regardless of the exact time, one day in our children's life time, the eight million mark will be reached.

When it is, how will our city look?

Many issues will need to be planned and resolved if Melbourne at eight million is to maintain its status as one of the World's Most Liveable Cities. We will need a vision for our future, much as Hoddle had a vision when he planned the CBD grid. Our vision will need to be equally as broad ranged as Hoddle's.

One of the many questions that we face in visioning Melbourne is: Where will all these people live?

Many people have a view on Docklands, some positive and some negative, but does the Docklands development provide us some lessons in determining *how* we plan, and *where* we plan, future growth?

Take Fisherman's Bend for example. Surely we could extend Docklands all through there?

Fisherman's Bend, the area separating the south bank of the Yarra from Port Melbourne is, when looking only at the map, ideally placed for residential development. Tell me Web Dock would not be a great place to live, surrounded on three sides by water?

Currently it is a giant car park.

Closer to the CBD than St. Kilda, potentially more accessible than Footscray, surrounded by great suburban locations, yet Fisherman's Bend is made up of light industrial lands.

There are reasons for this. Some industries went in back in the days when Fisherman's Bend was to be Melbourne's airport. Some industry is there to service the Port. Some industry is there as the Garden City area of Port Melbourne, where I did a paper round as a kid, was envisaged as a cheap dormitory area for the industrial workers. Now the prices have gone up and many of those working in Fisherman's Bend have long commutes.

The vision of close housing and work no longer applies, due to changes in area based demographics.

However, major decisions need to be made before Fisherman's Bend could be a great new Docklands.

Where would the Industry such as Holden go? How could we cost effectively move the different industries and employers without risking jobs and production? How would we clean up the contaminated land and who would pay for it? Where would you put the Port?

Clearly, if we take a short and a medium term vision, say five to 20 years, the cost effectiveness of a conversion of Fisherman's Bend would not stack up. We would leave it as an industrial area and try to find other interim solutions for a growing population.

But what of the longer term vision? What of Melbourne at eight million?

When planning a major city, or the significant growth of a major city, a long term comprehensive vision is surely more likely to lead to a better city, than short term ad-hoc responses, or medium term incremental changes.

We do not argue that Fisherman's Bend could provide the entire solution, or only solution, to a growing Melbourne. Nor does the Committee for Melbourne put forward the view that Fisherman's Bend *must* become residential.

Our point is more subtle than that. Our point is that many other growth options open up, many other solutions can be found, when a long term visionary approach is taken to planning Melbourne. Short and medium term plans don't give us exciting options for moving forward, geographically, economically, culturally and socially.

In a series of Shaping Melbourne Reports, the Committee for Melbourne this year will engage the community to look more at Density, Infrastructure, Community and Governance and will ask us all to look at the vision.

Above all our series of reports will call upon all of us Melbournians to engage in that 'Vision thing'. If we get the vision right, we get the city right. If we don't get the vision right then we get whatever just happens to come to pass.

Part Four: Selected Speeches and Miscellaneous

Order of Australia Association Speech

Introduction

I was asked to give a congratulatory speech to new recipients of the Order of Australia award in 2010. This is the transcript of that speech and it touches on issues of our national future.

Address to the Order of Australia Association (Victoria Branch)

Andrew McLeod CEO, Committee for Melbourne

Wednesday 22 September 2010 Melbourne Town Hall

Thank you very much and it is a great pleasure to be here today, but I have to say this is without doubt, one of the most imposing audiences I have ever been asked to speak in front of – this is not a room full of boring people. This is a room full of people who have achieved and given back to their community, their country and their people in many different incredible ways and it is indeed humbling to try and somehow speak to you about things that we can do in achieving in the community when all of you in this room have far exceeded anything that I have done or given. So for me it is a very humbling honour to speak in front of you.

For the new awardees, allow me, in my small way to also add my congratulations to you. You have been honoured by our community as a point of thanks for the work that you have done in very many different fields and I would like to also, as an Australian, extend my thanks for the work that you have done in your communities.

But given the introduction of my background, one of the questions you may be asking may be 'Why Melbourne? Why have you come back here?' And indeed I took on the role of Chief Executive Officer of the Committee for Melbourne back in January and this very question was asked of me by the Board, when interviewing prospective candidates for this role and they asked me 'Andrew, why do you want to come back to Melbourne?' and I said 'Honestly, there are two reasons. One, you can drink water from the tap and two, you have the MCG.'

And the Board said to me: 'You're being a bit flippant, aren't you?' and I said 'No, think about it for just a second. Drinking water from the tap. Eighty per cent of people on this planet – can't.' The fact that we can walk up to a tap in our apartments or houses and turn it on and get fresh, potable water every day puts us in the wealthiest people in the world. It says a lot about our infrastructure, it says a lot about our community, it says a lot about our governance. At the end of the day, this country works. And I find it completely bizarre that people go to restaurants and ask for a bottle of San Pelligrino and pay five bucks when, you can go to your tap and you can get the world's greatest luxury.

And I got my water bill the other day and do you know what it cost me for three months' of potable water pumped to my apartment? Fresh, clean, on demand whenever I wanted it? Thirteen dollars. For three months. It's insane. We don't price our water right, it doesn't reflect what a luxury it is, and I always make a point and I ask you too, from now on as well, whenever you are in a restaurant, don't ask for San Pelligrino – ask for tap water, because that's a luxury and we really need to appreciate those common, everyday things.

The second thing – the MCG. Now I'm a Collingwood supporter so I'm really scared about Saturday. And there's a difference between the older Collingwood supporters and the younger ones. The younger ones have got the lid off. 'We're going to win, we're going to win.' The older ones just list you dates: 1970, 1977, 1979, 1980, 1981, 2000, 2002, 2003 – we know how to lose Grand Finals.

But the thing about the MCG is, where else in the world can you put 80, 90, 100,000 people into a stadium, mix them all up together, and at the end of the day, someone wins and someone loses and everyone will go home without violence, without flares and without riots.

I was sitting at the Collingwood Geelong game about Round 3 or 4 this year – and it was round about the time of the Super Profits Tax – now I'm not going to talk about whether that's a right thing or not a right thing, but I was with a group of Collingwood supporters and the row in front was a group of Geelong supporters. So of course during the first and second quarter we're having that friendly banter with each other – 'No, it wasn't a push in the back.' Oh yes, he had it…etc, etc..'

Then at half time the bloke in front turned around and said to me 'What do you think of the Super Profits Tax?' And I gave my view. We had a great discussion. Then the third quarter started and we were back hammering each other again.

Where else in the world, does that sort of thing happen and the greatest thing about the MCG if you ask me, is not during the game but it is at the end. And if you go this weekend, at the end of the game, have a look around as people are leaving. Have a look at how many 12 –13 – 14 year olds are in groups – unsupervised. Where else in the world, could a 14 year old girl, rock up to Mum and Dad and say 'I'm going to a mass public event with a hundred thousand people and no adult supervision' and Mum says 'See you when you get home.'

So – the MCG says a lot about our community. How we relate and interact with each other. The respect that we pay for each other and at the end of the day what a great society and community, Melbourne is.

So those two simple things, drinking water from the tap and the MCG say a lot about our community, our governance, our infrastructure and how well we get on – and at the end of the day, all of us in the MCG, or in this room, are in the top half of the top 1% of wealthy and privileged people in the world. The thing that makes you special is you've recognised that and you've given back to your community – and what we need to continue to do, is spread that knowledge of how good a life and society that we have in Melbourne and what an obligation that imposes upon us in whatever way we can, in whatever strengths we have, to give back to our community around us.

Which brings me to the Committee for Melbourne. What is the Committee for Melbourne and why would I come back for this role? The Committee for Melbourne was founded in 1985. It brings together the biggest businesses and organisations of Melbourne to do networking activities and gives policy advice to government to keep Melbourne the world's most liveable city. It is 100% private sector funded. It is a way of businesses and organisations, collectively, giving back to the community around them.

Historically, what have we been doing, what are we involved with? Well we brought the designers of London's docklands out to Melbourne, back in '85 to have a look at our docklands which brought about the redesign and the reconstruction of Docklands, the free City Circle tram came from the Committee for Melbourne, some green roofs programs – for gardens on the stop of our CBD buildings came out of the Committee for Melbourne, the bud lighting on Collins Street and Swanston Street came out of the Committee for Melbourne. So I'd like to say that the Committee for Melbourne does everything from changing light bulbs to changing suburbs and everything in between.

It is an organisation which allows us to sit around a table and turn the 'they' into the 'we' – instead of talking about 'they' (whomever that is) doing something about this or that problem, we say 'No, we'll do it.' Bringing the collective views, opinions, knowledge and capacity of the private sector and its staff, to get things done.

So what are we doing at the moment? What is important for us, looking forward to the future?

Well, we believe that Dick Smith is the greatest threat to the future of the ability of major cities in Australia. Why? He promotes this vision that we can cap the population growth of our cities, and we should cap the population growth of our cities. Why do we see this as dangerous? Not even the most autocratic governments in the world can cap their population. Many have tried. The fact that whether you want it or not, whether you think it is a good idea or not, you can't actually do it. It is not possible, particularly in a free and democratic society, to cap our population.

Our population growth comes from three places. Interstate migration, international migration and natural reproduction. Let's have a look at these three – for to cap our population, we would need to cap all three.

Can we cap interstate migration? Well, our Constitution guarantees freedom of movement between States. The only way we could cap interstate migration is if we made Melbourne ugly, and that's not a good idea.

International Migration: Can we cap international migration? Well, technically, legally - yes, we could. Is it a good idea? No. Hands up – and bear with me for a moment – who here is not Australian born? Now just take a look around the room at the hands. Do we really want to exclude future generations of this sort of percentage of people who give to our community from all over the world by capping, stopping international migration? Absolutely not.

And thirdly, natural reproduction. 0.6% of our population growth which is about 1.9% in Melbourne comes from natural reproduction. Pray tell, how do we cap that? Therefore it is a fiction to say that we could cap our population growth, no matter how attractive an idea it may seem.

So why is Dick Smith such a threat? If he wins the public discourse debate and somehow we get the general population to believe that you can cap population growth, how do we invest in roads, public transport, hospitals and schools we need for the future if every time a politician says we need to spend 'x' number of dollars on this piece of infrastructure and the general population says 'Hang on, we didn't want to grow.' We would find ourselves in twenty or thirty years' time with a city that does have a growing population because we can't cap those three factors but we haven't built the infrastructure, the roads, the schools, the hospitals and things we need.

For the Committee for Melbourne, one of the most important things for us to have on our agenda is that it is much better to plan for growth and slow that implementation down if growth doesn't happen than it is to pretend that growth isn't happening and then try and catch up afterwards.

If we want to give our children a more congested and a more polluted future let's pretend we're not going to grow. If we want to give our children a less congested and a less polluted future then let's plan for the challenges that growth brings – and this is what the Committee for Melbourne is doing.

I've put up on the table just a sample of the current series of reports we are doing on shaping Melbourne. There are only five or six copies up there but it is downloadable from our website if you are interested in the policy debate about the future for Melbourne. Very easy website: www.melbourne.org.au but we are also, as the Committee for Melbourne, one of the guardians of brand image 'Melbourne'. We look out for threats to brand image Melbourne, and opportunities for brand image Melbourne, and let me touch on each of those, just quickly.

Under the idea of threats, clearly one of the biggest threats to brand image Melbourne at the moment is the issue around violence and international students. Melbourne is not a violent city by any stretch of the imagination and I will go back to my comment about fourteen year old girls going to a mass public event and mum saying 'See you when you get home.'

We have a perception of violence in Melbourne that we need to fix. Part of it is that there is more violence than we would like in our community but by any global measures; we are one of the least violent societies in the world. And think about it, we see a lot of non-lethal violence on the front page of our newspapers and there are two reasons we have non-lethal violence on the front page of our newspapers. One is we have non-lethal violence, and we need to fine-tune our community and our society, to reduce that. The second reason we have non-lethal violence on the front page of our newspapers is that there is not enough 'lethal' violence to keep it off.

It's actually a measure of success of how mild an event makes the front page of our newspapers. Would non-lethal violence make the front of The New York Times? No. Would it make the front page of the London Times? No, let alone the Islamabad Gazette, let along Kigali, let alone Manila, let alone Colombo. So we sometimes need a bit of a reality check and do something that Australians are very, very bad at: that is self-congratulation.

We have managed to build a very good society, while we must fine-tune to keep improving, we must congratulate ourselves on what we've done well.

There is a very good line in the 'Shaping Melbourne Report' up on the table that starts, that says this 'Melbourne marks the beginning of its current rate of improvement from 1990 when we were voted the world's most liveable city.' Now I love that line, because it says a lot about how we measure ourselves. We don't measure ourselves against the top ten; we don't even measure ourselves against the top one. We mark the beginning of our improvement from when we were voted the world's best. In other words, we got there and said 'Right. Now how do we get better?'

And that's the on-going challenge we have in this society is to build on that strength that we have and continue to get better by being realistic about what we need to improve, and being realistic where we're already good.

So let's go back to the international students. We did a bit of a study and we noticed that most of the acts of violence against international students happen between a point of public transport and a point of part-time employment. And generally because people were walking across parks at midnight in Footscray.

Now in any major city in the world, you just don't do that. And one of the things that I have learnt in my life is when you are living and working in someone else's culture, you always, not sometimes, you always inadvertently make some sort of cultural *faux pas* that increases your vulnerability.

For me when I moved into Islamabad I found a gym around the corner from home and I thought 'Ripper!' whacked on the shoes, shorts and t-shirt and I went to do a jog to the gym to do a workout. I got half a block before the abuse turned me round. Because men didn't wear shorts in Islamabad. I knew women didn't but I didn't know that men didn't.

As my mother used to always tell me 'Andrew, everyone needs to be told everything at least once.'

So, who's telling these kids where it is safe to walk and where it's not in Melbourne? They've read all this bumf that it is safe and friendly with Melbourne being a wonderful city, which is true. But who's told them 'Don't walk across the park at midnight.'

Truthfully, the only person who can is the employer, because it must be site-specific. A safe access between point of public transport and point of employment must be done by the employer. So, together with the Victorian Employers' Chamber of Commerce and Industry, we've called in the main employers of international students, 7-Eleven, McDonalds, Woolworths, Taxi

213

Association and said 'What do you think about this? We should do it.' And the employers said 'You're right.'

So we're creating a voluntary Code of Conduct for the employment of international students to incorporate security and cultural awareness training as part of staff induction programs, flexibility around scheduling around exam periods and an undertaking to respect employment legislation.

That is a very good collaborative and cooperative approach to a problem. Here is a problem, identify where the real solution is, pull the people around the table and solve the problem. This is what the Committee for Melbourne is. It's a collection of bringing people together to solve problems but also to look out for opportunities.

Here is a really good one – Melbourne is the philanthropic corporate responsibility and humanitarian hub of Australia. We have just never said that.

We like to say we're Number One for sport, we're Number One for culture, we're Number One for food, we're Number One for shopping and if you listen to the Premier, he also says we're Number One for romance, but I am yet to see that.

But we are also Number One for corporate social responsibility, philanthropy and humanitarian affairs. And think about this, the big NGOs of Australia: Save the Children Australia, World Vision Australia, Australian Red Cross, Oxfam Australia, are all in Melbourne, not Canberra. The big philanthropic funds: Pratts, Smorgans, Myers are all in Melbourne, not Sydney. And the global corporate social responsibility of Rio, BHP, ANZ, NAB, Optus, Telstra, SKM and others are in Melbourne.

And we have this really interesting confluence of factors in history coming together today. One, we have a growing understanding of ineffectiveness and inefficiencies of the United Nations and large NGOs in international development, I've been in that game for a number of years, I can justify that statement.

Secondly, we have a growing professionalisation coming out of community investment and corporate sociability programs and thirdly, a growing demand from Generation Y to have a social outcome as part of their work.

214

This confluence point of three things, growing dissatisfaction with the public sector delivery mechanisms, growing confidence in the private sector delivery mechanisms and growing demand from Generation Y, means that the people who can understand this, the city, the town, the companies, that understand this first, can take a genuine global leadership position.

Melbourne is so well placed for this, because we are that philanthropic corporate social responsibility and humanitarian hub of Australia. So why don't we do something to make us a leader in the world at this. So we have. In the Committee for Melbourne, we've pulled together a little informal group, BHP, Rio, ANZ, NAB, Optus, Telstra, KPMG, SKM, Winston Young, Australia Post and the Myer Foundation. Between them there is 700 million dollars of annual development spending coming out of just those eleven organisations in the Committee for Melbourne.

BHP Billiton spends 1% of pre-tax profit on community investment programs globally, that's two hundred million US dollars a year, making them the third largest development agency in Australia, bigger than the Red Cross. Five companies at the global level, the size of BHP spend one billion dollars. That's the same budget as the United Nations Development Program. In other words, it only takes five big companies to spend the same amount of money on development as the international organisation we rely on to bring the world out of poverty.

The top one hundred in the world spend fifteen billion dollars. That's the same budget as the entire United Nations system, including all peace keeping and security affairs. As a market it is estimated at being fifty-nine billion dollars a year.

Now, Miss World says that we want everyone to be friendly and peaceful and kind to animals, I think that we actually have a way of doing it. And I think we can do it in Melbourne.

I think that we can build off the goodwill that exists within the private sector, within our philanthropic organisations, within groups like the ones I'm sure many of you had participated in, and instead of just being the Australian leader, let's be the global leader. Let's, over the next few years, build Melbourne to be the private sector version of Geneva. Where we can have a meaningful impact on the world, into the future and have the same impact upon Melbourne as putting the Red Cross in Geneva in 1859.

And let me put this to you, why is the Red Cross in Geneva? Many people say, when I ask this question, 'Ah, it's because Switzerland is neutral.' Actually, it's the other way around. In 1859 Switzerland, as we now know it hadn't fully confederated and the fact that the Red Cross was in Geneva, created a mentality of neutrality that created the entire national culture that then brought the League of Nations to Geneva after World War I – that created the United Nations Headquarters in Geneva after World War II. That's the impact of a vision.

If we get this right in Melbourne, what can we do for this city over the next fifty or one hundred years? It's a great convergence point in history and we have an enormous opportunity to grab it.

Let me now; be just slightly self-indulgent for a moment. I would like to stray from what I was asked to talk about to pay my respects to a man who should have been here.

Many of you will know Tony Hewison AM. He received his Order of Australia for services to education. He died two weeks ago.

He was my best friend's father. He was my headmaster; he was a life-mentor and a lifetime friend. In the last Speech Night that he gave as Headmaster of St Michael's Grammar, he set a list of characteristics by which you should measure one's life. Now I'm sure that many of you would agree with, and live by this list. The list that he gave to students should set their lives is this:

One should have: personal integrity, total honesty, love for others, moral courage and a courage to speak out when others are silent, you should take responsibility for yourself and for your actions, you should have perseverance and endurance, the acceptance of the rough with the smooth, personal obligation, doing one's duty as well as proclaiming one's rights, maintaining enquiring minds, and seeking lives free of empty cant, a sense of community as well as a declaration of individuality, self-confidence and a healthy pride, respect for others and humility and above all, a willingness to learn.

It's a very strong list of great characteristics that Tony lived by all of his life and passed on to many of the students that were under his care. Tony was a worthy Order of Australia recipient, and it is of great sadness to me that he is not here today when he should have been.

So I would like to finish by saying Tony was a great person, the characteristics are what we need in our citizens and they are the characteristics that many of you have clearly shown in your lives and your work. So in thanking Tony, I would also like to thank you for your work for Australia. Thank you.

Richard Searby Oration

I was asked to deliver the 2011, Richard Searby Oration for Deakin University on Tuesday, 27 September 2011. Below is a transcript of that speech.

Multimedia (ebook only)
Extracts from the speech are available on video here and the full speech here.

Better To Light A Candle Than Curse The Darkness
Good evening ladies and gentlemen and thank you for taking your time tonight to celebrate and honour Dr Searby.

It is a great honour and privilege to give the Richard Searby Oration for 2011. Dr Searby's life has been one marked by achievement, a thirst for knowledge and service to the community. From his early days schooled by his father, to working as Associate to Sir Owen Dixon, his work as a leading member of the legal profession and his latter days as Chancellor, Dr Searby has never lost the great respect for knowledge and ideas.

To Dr Searby it is the role of universities to expand the global pool of knowledge and encourage discussion and discourse – hence it is fitting that an annual Oration is named in his honour.

I believe Australia is a good country.

For most of the last 15 years, I have had the great privilege of working for the United Nations and the International Committee of the Red Cross in some of the world's most difficult situations.

In the earliest of those years, I felt filled with pride by how others referred to Australia. Seen as an open and tolerant country, Australia was an example of the society that had the balance right.

Over more recent years, people couldn't quite reconcile the openness of our society with how our national dialogue appeared to have changed.

Over the last year or so, many of us here would have lamented the quality of our political debate. But given we are a democracy ultimate responsibility for the quality of debate and discourse does not rest with politicians, nor the media.

It rests with us, the Australian people. The voters.

The challenge I will put tonight is this: we must take a role in lifting the quality of debate. We must make a change each time we are engaged in discussions around policy, be it at work, or with family and friends. We must rise and encourage a race to the top of the mountain, not to the bottom of the barrel.

I still believe that ours is a good country, made up of people who care for the nation's future.

I have always felt that.

In 1994, I had the good fortune to be sitting opposite a young man who became a great friend, Rufus Black, in a small pizza shop in Princeton New Jersey. Rufus and I were studying postgraduate degrees in the UK, he at Oxford and me at a less well known institution to the south.

Back those 17 years, knowing what I wanted to do internationally, Rufus asked me why I didn't want to work in Australia.

"Because Rufus," I said, "at the end of the day I have inherent faith that the Australian people get it right."

Fast forward to 2001, immediately following that year's Tampa election, Rufus called me and asked if I still held that view.

I questioned it then, and I question it now. Do we, as a nation, collectively get it right?

The science of politics maybe of sound bites and tweets, but the art of politics must be to inspire, not the cynical manipulation in the pursuit of electoral power.

If the phrase 'cynical manipulation' sounds too strong or confronting, could I insert one of: 'overuse of focus groups', 'sound bite responses', 'twitter feeds' or 'Facebook updates' in its place?

Cast your mind back 10 years. While many, including some in this room, may have agreed with the focus group driven statement "we decide who comes to our country and the circumstances in which they come", there was at that time an opposing view on the opposite side of the parliamentary chamber. Some even on the then government side.

Without agreeing with one side or the other in that debate, at least I can say there was a debate.

Oh how that has changed. I now want to put the Challenge to you:

We decide who leads our country and the circumstances in which they lead!

Let me ask you this: If back in 2001, we were told that within ten years our country would be led by a female prime minister from the left wing of the Labor Party, who promoted off-shore processing as the refugee solution in Australia – you would rightly have said that maybe one of those four things would come true.

Many have said that the refugee issue should not be a big issue. And I agree. It should not be. But it is.

This issue has now moved beyond one of boats. It has moved beyond the location of processing. It has even moved beyond one of people.

This has grown now to become an issue about the soul of our country, an issue about the content of our collective character. It is now a debate about who we are and how we wish to be perceived.

Former Villawood manager, Peter Mitchel, wrote in his just released book "Compassionate Bastard" that:

"(we) have to accept the fact that the refugee issue is complex and defies a quick fix. Asylum seekers will continue to arrive by boat. And politicians have to stop oversimplifying the issue by trying to outdo one another with tough talk."

We are an intelligent country that can engage in difficult debate. Having worked for the UNHCR, I know the issue is complicated. Mitchel is right, the asylum debate is difficult and it does our country no good to simply say 'stop the boats'.

But nor does it do justice to a complicated issue to say 'just let them land'. Any policy that in any way encourages people to jump on leaky boats to undertake a risky voyage with a high likelihood of death, is a bad policy.

It is not the purpose of this oration to suggest a refugee solution. It is the purpose to call for a lifting of the quality of national discourse. Our country should be known as one that debates in detail, not sound bites.

Can I suggest a three point framework to guide detailed debate around refugees by way of example?

A. Any policy must have the best humanitarian solution for asylum seekers as its driving focus, those here, those seeking to come and those waiting elsewhere for resettlement.

B. Any policy must satisfy legitimate concerns for border security.

C. Any policy must enhance and not detract from Australia's international reputation.

I would suggest the framework of humanitarian, legitimate concern and image as a good guide to judge alternative policy suggestions.

If we do this it becomes clear that the question we are currently debating; the one of location of processing – Australia, Malaysia or Nauru is the wrong one. The harder and more critical issue is that of resettlement once a refugee is processed.

The back of the people smugglers business model is not one of the location of processing; it is a lack of resettlement after processing.

The Bali Process, and the Regional Cooperation Framework it created, is a good start to regionally discuss the plethora of complicated issues from trafficking, to law enforcement and permanent solutions for asylum seekers. The government should be credited for trying to make that process work. However this forum could be used more to search for lasting solutions on resettlement and those resettlement issues should be the main focus of Australia's involvement, not location of processing.

I readily admit this is complex, but in today's Australia complex issues are not framed in a way we can, as a community, digest. We are given sound bites.

Ask yourself if you are comfortable with the way our political debate is framed in Australia?

Ask yourself if the framing of debate is generating good or bad policy outcomes?

Ask yourself if the framing of debate is shaping an image and reputation of which we are proud?

Are we a country that seeks deep analysis before deciding complex issues? One that is inspired by the positive? Or one that looks to sound bites and seeks energy from the negative? Do we have genuine alternatives from which we are asked to choose?

Gone are the days of discourse surrounding great issues like conscription, urban planning, floating the dollar. Back then we were given alternative visions, alternative views

Back then, we had politicians who would put ideas on the table. We had 'recessions we had to have' and 'banana republics'. We had ideas we agreed with, and ideas that we disagreed with. We had vision and challenges put before us.

We were inspired to choose.

Today, the issues are not gone. But the visionaries have fallen quiet.

Take carbon emissions. It is a major issue. I find it disconcerting that I know more about the so-called disaster that will befall our country if carbon tax is introduced, or the ineffectiveness of direct action, than I do positives of either program.

I am being asked today, more often than not, to vote against a fear, than for a vision.

This state of affairs does not sit comfortably with me.

This is a problem statement that many share and express, but what about a solution?

I started by saying we all need to step up and improve discourse. I mean we all need to, in whichever way we feel comfortable. Lamenting without action is just not enough.

Let me move to four issues that while divergent; demonstrate an interesting trend of long-term thinking developing in the business sector: planning, natural disaster recovery, international education and international aid. Although different, these issues all share some hope of new thinking.

Planning

Melbourne has just been voted the world's most liveable city. How to keep it that way?

It is possible to have a small village congested and dirty if planned and administered badly. Likewise, it is possible to have a large city which is clean and fluid if planned and administered well. It doesn't come down to size, it's all about planning.

So, where is our long-term vision for this great city?

Committee for Melbourne is calling for a 50 year plan for Melbourne, based on a logical analysis of where our population will be. Not necessarily a population figure we are encouraging or discouraging, but one we are planning for – there is a distinct difference.

Only when we have a planning figure, can we plan the roads, the schools, and the infrastructure we need for a growing city.

The Committee believes growth will slow from 1.65% (our 50 year average) to around 1.4% over the next 50 years.

But even a slowing growth rate will see Melbourne get to around eight million people by 2060. This number causes fear, and fear deters our political leaders from engaging in long-term discourse.

Making Melbourne more liveable with that number is possible, but only if we plan it, discuss it and bring the community on board. Only if we plan to make Melbourne better in the future, rather than hoping we will not grow, will we succeed in giving to our children an even better city than the one given to us by our parents.

And this is why we have in the past been quoted as saying that Dick Smith is a threat to the future liveability of Australian cities.

We do so because we believe his calls distract public debate from one of planning of infrastructure – issues we can 100% control – and have people concentrating on planning population – an issue we can fine tune at best.

We don't believe Dick has malicious intent, we just believe that the debate is in the wrong place.

We should plan for the population that we think we will have, and build the infrastructure that population needs.

When did you last hear a politician give a 50 year view for Melbourne, like Menzies once did, like Whitlam once did? We remember Whitlam's Family Law Act, Medicare and The Dismissal, but do we equally remember the building of sewers in the outer suburbs and investment in infrastructure?

Whilst we may think Dick Smith is wrong, we would not try to silence him. He helps encourage debate when others are silent.

But this debate should be led by political leaders, not a retired business man on one hand, and the CEO of Committee for Melbourne on the other. There should not be a vacuum in the first place for us to fill.

But there is a spark of hope here in Melbourne. We have in our new Planning Minister, Matthew Guy, a man who says the impacts of his decisions will not be felt in his time in the Planning Ministry, nor his party's time in government, but in 20 or 30 years. If planning questions are debated, and planning decisions are made, in this timeframe, it will be a great step forward.

I have a vision of a city in 50 years that is more liveable than the one we have today: A city with a fully integrated public and private transport system.

I would like us to remove Melbourne's rail level crossings. With 172 of them, we cannot put more trains on our network without having the level crossings close more often and thereby clog up our roads. Melbourne is at a city-wide, system-wide, mobility crisis point that the last two governments failed to address. It is time to remove the level crossings – yet it will cost $17 billion to do so. We need to discuss this.

I would like us to stop the unsustainable decreasing density in this city. With the highest average footprint house in the world, with less people per house as our family sizes shrink, we are continuing to spread, from a density of 23 people per hectare in 1960, to around about 14 today.

Consider this, by 2025, 51% of households in Melbourne will be 'no child' households (pre, post or decided to have no children). So why are we building so many family homes?

This is the dialogue we need to have, but only if we have a logical discussion on where our population is likely to be. Who is leading this logical discussion today?

Post disaster

Dorothy MacKellar told us when she was just 19, that Australia is the land of droughts and flooding rains. We know also that we are the land of fires and cyclones. For years, we have built up some of the globe's best immediate response teams, if not policy. The Red Cross. SES. CFA. Emergency Management Australia (EMA), an organisation most Australian's don't know of, has worked over the years to ensure lessons learned and interoperability on emergency response.

But why is it that, our national leaders seem to plan for good immediate response, but still do post-disaster recovery and reconstruction in an ad hoc way?

Why do we have the Victorian Bushfire Reconstruction Authority set up for one event? Why did it need to re-learn the lessons of Cyclone Larry, rather than have an institution that had learned in advance? Why did Queensland establish yet another ad hoc mechanism to deal with the floods, and why do we need a flood levy?

We are told that the answer to all these questions is a version of 'well this was unforeseen.'

I only need to go back to that great fortune teller, Dorothy MacKellar, to seek guidance. We know for sure that in my lifetime disaster will happen again – many times. After all, in my life time so far, the 'rare' events have included Cyclones Tracey, Larry and others, Black Saturday fires, Ash Wednesday, two great floods in Queensland, a couple in Melbourne, and whole bunch of droughts.

In the last six months, I have lobbied Federal and State, Labor and Liberal MPs, around one very simple issue:

If we are the land of droughts and flooding rains, and if we have our act together well enough to be one of the world's best at emergency response, why do we still do recovery in an ad hoc way?

Why can't we slightly extend the mandate of EMA to include lessons learned and share knowledge on recovery as well as response? All but four politicians gave me a bunch of reasons why it couldn't happen.

Credit to Simon Crean, Andrew Robb, Janelle Saffin and Greg Hunt for seeing an alternative. Two are in power, two may soon be. Let's see if a simple and cheap idea can become policy.

IBM is about to hold a Colloquium here in Melbourne and this is how this multi-national sees it:

We are witnessing the largest wave of urban growth in history with more than 50% of the world's population now living in cities. We have also witnessed the incredible power of nature during the

2011. The intersection of major disasters, with increased population density and the interconnectedness of our businesses and economies, is leading to a requirement for communities, organisations, cities and countries to become more resilient. This colloquium will explore our vulnerability, preparedness and responsiveness to large-scale events, and what opportunities exist to improve societal resilience.

Why is it that business is doing this not government? Why does business see the long-term impact, but all but a few political leaders can't?

International education

Recent ABS statistics revealed a drop in population growth from 2.2% to 1.5%.

As natural increase has stayed relatively level, this drop is a result of a dive in net overseas migration - largely from international students. Whilst some may be relieved on the easing of pressure on our infrastructure, is this drop really a good or bad thing for Melbourne and Australia?

Education is Melbourne's second largest and formerly largest export. It is a larger export earner to Australia than gold, natural gas, wheat, and even beef. International education is so big that Deloitte Access Economics equates it to around 1% of GDP; providing around 100,000 jobs to the economy, or about one job for every two higher education students in Australia.

Put another way, for every two international students lost, we lose one Australian job. Roughly 20% of the impact being in retail.

The fall in international students has seen a drop of nearly 23,000 students in 2011. That is 11,500 Australian jobs lost.

If the current drop is not cause for alarm, then the future projections to 2015 should be. By 2015, some forecasts predict a drop of nearly 70,000 students against future expectations. If this occurs, it would mean 35,000 fewer Australian jobs in the broader economy.

So why are we not strongly fighting to protect this industry?

Rather than being concerned about jobs, for some reason our nation appears so fearful on population growth that we applaud the drop in arrivals without fully understanding the broader economic impact.

Glenn Withers, the chief of Universities Australia said that the negativity surrounding Australian public debate on population, migration and refugees is "creating an impression that we are not welcoming students, or even welcoming visitors."

We must work urgently to reverse the negative brand image of Australia as unwelcoming because it is untrue.

We should not be surprised by this brand image risk.

We had 30 years notice.

Recently released papers revealed discussions in the Fraser Cabinet. Michael Mackellar, the then Immigration Minister said to the cabinet:

"Under international law Australia could legislate to: prohibit entry to Australian territorial seas, to vessels carrying refugees and expel such vessels. In view of our image as a developed, technologically advanced and still under-populated country, such steps would be courting international pariah status."

This was said 30 years ago. This was why we had a positive narrative at that time. I see no reason why today, we should have a different reasoning from that which applied over 30 years ago. We are still risking pariah status. The risk appears to manifest itself in the education sector.

As global uncertainty envelopes all industries, we must not see the international education sector as an isolated victim, rather, we should see it as a strong indicator of threats to the broader economy. It would be naive to think otherwise.

Those involved in business, small, medium and large know that good reputation is critical. When given a choice, people prefer to do business with people they like. It is human nature.

If the international education sector is the canary in the cage, and if the framing of national debate on population, refugees and immigration is portraying Australia as an 'unwelcoming' country, there is no doubt this will impact the broader economy and cost Australian jobs.

We know business is starting to realise this because more and more business leaders are speaking out to protect Australia's brand image. Who would have thought only ten years ago, some of the most pro-refugee and pro-immigrant voices were not the left wing, but some of our business leaders?

Then there is a deeper issue: Surely if we want to improve the globe, enhance inter-cultural dialogue and understanding, reduce conflict, enhance collaboration and cooperation, isn't international education a great diplomatic tool, not just an economic benefit?

Let me propose two simple policy ideas:

1. Every Australian Embassy in the South East and South Asian regions should foster the creation of an "Australian Alumni". Many senior political and business leaders in the Asia Pacific region have received some or all of their education in Australia. We should maximise the diplomatic, cultural and business advantages to all countries by keeping track and fostering a lifetime cultural connection between former students and our country. While some universities are doing this, surely the Australian government should do so as part of a soft diplomatic outreach.

2. We should allow Australian businesses that are looking to expand into the region to employ students upon graduation in Australia. We should allow them a year or two to understand the culture of the business and then be beach-head staff employed back in their home countries by our companies, thereby allowing the Australian business to have a better chance to thrive. The Knight review released last week is heading in this direction and has recommended changes to the visa rules to allow this. The government has indicated that they will accept that recommendation, and I look forward to it becoming law.

International Aid

Let me go to a final area: international aid.

Fifty three per cent of capital flows from the OECD countries to the developing world are through private sector. Only 17% are through aid.

While UN Development Program's core funding is $1 billion a year (there is more in noncore funding), the combined CSR spend of Committee for Melbourne Members alone is $1.5 billion. The top 100 companies in the world spend $15 billion – the same as the entire UN budget.

BHP Billiton spends 1% of pre-tax profit on community engagement. That is $220 million a year - making BHP the world largest miner, fifth largest company in the world and the third largest development agency in Australia. Even larger than the Australian Red Cross.

So why is business doing this?

In Mozal Mozambique, BHP Billiton runs an anti-malaria campaign that has seen adult infections drop from around 82% of the population to 8%. Their internal documents state a major reason for doing the campaign is to help achieve the Millennium Development Goals. Think on that.

But there is an additional benefit.

The improved community health has seen absenteeism in the workforce drop from 22% to 2%, improving the productivity of their assets by an amount higher than the cost of the entire program.

People may be tempted to say "see, they only do it for profit." I say, the link with profit is not a bad thing, as it guarantees the long-term viability of the project.

Win, win, win.

When you speak to some senior business leaders like Karen Wood at BHP, Bruce Harvey at Rio, Julie Bisinella at ANZ, you are left in no doubt that their objective is to find ways where their companies can genuinely improve the communities in which they operate. It is not just for profit. In the long run it is, in their view, the right thing to do.

And here is the key: The companies are thinking long-term. Not in twitter feeds. Not in electoral cycles.

Listening to people who have successfully invested and built business in China, in the region - I hear them say - Embrace, engage, learn, immerse, exchange our expertise in our region. They don't say protect, beware, control, change or stop. They say 'yes', not 'no'.

It is perhaps an unusual position to look to business as a source of inspiration in today's Australia. But business is only just coming to terms with this itself. It is new ground. There is a lot to learn and improve. And yes, there is a lot to analyse between market motivations and community motivations.

I am not saying by any means that corporations are perfect, many are far from that. But leading companies are making some efforts and we need to give credit where credit is due.

Let me leave those four examples of unusual thinking in planning, disaster recovery, education and aid, and return to the larger problem.

I am yet to meet the person who says to me:

"That last federal election was truly inspiring. I was uplifted with a sense of confidence in our national leaders and a feeling of 'relaxed comfortableness'."

I am yet to meet *that* person. More lament the lack of those feelings. But we lament more often in silence.

Ronald Reagan building on Burke's sentiments beseeched people to:

"Stand up for what is right or sit back and let evil prevail."

I agree with Reagan, not on all his views, but certainly upon that.

His view that one should not just sit back, is neither new nor restricted to western societies. There is an old Chinese proverb:

"Better to light a candle than curse the darkness."

Lapse of leadership is the darkness. We must demand leadership and by doing so enhance quality debate. Quality debate is the light of the candle. "Better to light a candle than curse the darkness."

This proverb transcends all nations and cultures. This proverb should inspire us to realise that the apparent lapse of leadership is not Australia's burden carried in isolation. Those dynamics of twitter, focus groups and endless news cycles, do not manifest themselves in Australia alone. If you doubt that, can I suggest you have a cup of tea in the United States just now?

If the problem is global, can a solution begin locally? Is it possible for Australia to be a leading light rather than a following deputy?

Australia, as a nation lacking a burden of colonial expansionist history, and a nation rightly absent a belief that its culture is big enough to dominate the world by force, has in many times in its history sought to assert its influence, in the words of Barack Obama:

"By asserting not the example of our power but the power of our example."

And what an example we are: living in the world's most liveable city, in the second most liveable country on earth. Perhaps our greatest failing is not recognising how much we get right. Simple things like watching groups of 12, 13 and 14 year olds leaving the MCG after a football match. Ask yourself, where else in the world could a 14 year old girl say to her mum: 'Hi mum, I am going to a mass public event with 100,000 people and no adult supervision,' and mum replies, 'See you when you get home dear'?

Where else could this happen? Do we realise how good our society is, and therefore, how hard we must fight to protect it?

Oh how it would be if our leaders were like the Norwegian Prime Minister, who in addressing his nation following those dreadful attacks earlier this year, held no fear in showing emotion, confusion and bewilderment at the assault. But he still stood firm in the resolute belief that one deranged person would not derail the openness of his society.

Whilst leadership through history is in some ways cyclical, with periods of greatness and periods of tenuity, we should hope for the former.

I worked with Shaukut Aziz in Pakistan. He is a fine man and an example of a fine leader. He did remarkable things as both Pakistan's Finance Minister and Prime Minister in circumstance so difficult that most couldn't even imagine. He was a deserving winner of the 2001 award.

In leadership one remembers that no-one has the monopoly on good ideas, and no-one is always wrong. It is therefore worth listening to other's ideas, and we should encourage leaders that can applaud with us the good ideas of their opposition.

Hawke was a master of this.

We all must demand of our leaders, who give credit where credit is due, build on other's good ideas, in order to inspire us to choose between strong and stronger, not fear and fright. We used to have such leaders.

Men and women who spoke of lights on hills also held visions of a community of nations ridding the earth of the scourge that is war. They lead using the strength of the example of this nation.

We were a leading people in the establishment of the United Nations, fights against apartheid, in support of boat people, in recognition of China.

We lead from this nation by the power of our example.

Paul Keating described Malcolm Fraser thus:

"The unifying theme behind all Fraser's foreign policy was a pragmatic and independent search for the Australian national interest. When speaking for Australia abroad he was consistently informed, formidable and constructive."

It takes character to give credit to an opponent. It takes leadership to set a moral course.

We lost that with Tampa.

When we were asked those 11 years ago, "Do we want those types of people here", why could we not have said:

"People willing to risk their lives and work hard for nothing more than the better future for their children? Yes we want them here!"

Wouldn't it be better if our national dialogue was one of how to accept a fair share here in a controlled and fair manner, rather than how to keep people away? A 'controlled entry program' rather than 'border protection'?

Tampa was for this nation a turning point. It is when we stopped leading on the basis of hope and optimism and started inspiring through fear.

Tampa began a change in our national culture, it challenged our national character and we are yet to undo that damage.

I, like many here, hunger and thirst for positive dialogue, intelligent dialogue, challenging dialogue.

In the words of Bobby Kennedy:

"Each time a man stands up for an ideal, or acts to improve the lot of the rest or strikes out against injustice, he sends forth a tiny ripple of hope, and crossing each other from millions of centres of energy and daring, those ripples build a current that can sweep down the mightiest walls of oppression and resistance …

Few are willing to brave the disapproval of their fellows, the censure of their colleagues, the wrath of their society. Moral courage is a rarer commodity than bravery in battle or great intelligence. Yet it is the one essential, vital quality for those who seek to change a world that yields most painfully to change."

That is a big, inspiring statement and we as a country can be as big as that.

In preparing tonight's Oration, I shared the draft text with a few people of different ages, and sought feedback.

One friend in her mid 20's friend from a politically active family emailed me and said:

"I think that for many young people my age it is not just that there is a lack of vision and leadership among our politicians; it is that they no longer believe that politics or politicians can actually achieve real change...

As a result of this we have become not just politically disengaged from the main parties, but from the very issues they are actually debating..."

Disagreement is one thing, disengagement is worse. How bad will the future of our country be if we have a generation that doesn't even think the debate is worth entering?

A friend at the older end of the spectrum responding saying:

It seems to be that much discussion and action in the public domain lacks any generosity of spirit, indeed there is almost a grinding meanness to debate. Business seems to have grasped this, and in order to survive, has seized on rewarding loyalty as one of the key motivators to maintain custom. Enlightened self-interest? Of course. Good for all? Yes. Far-sighted? Yes.
So, back to solutions again.

Lindsay Tanner nearly got it right when he blamed the media.

Let me put a refined view.

We, as the consumers and creators of media, must demand leaders frame the content of the debate in a way that strengthens the content of our national character: To give us not a choice of fear, but a choice of hope.

When we read, or hear ourselves repeat the negativity, remember the first step on rectification is to rectify ourselves.

New media, new groups energised around issues and hope are tools that can be used to build much deeper community dialogue, not shorter sound bites. New media tools should be an opportunity for politicians to engage in longer dialogue of substance. There is hope with GetUp and other like mechanisms, but we need to demand it. The responsibility is ours.

If you agree with me that we have a vacuum in quality political discourse in planning, immigration, emergency aid, education, global poverty, or whatever else drives your passion, then you have two choices: sit back and lament the darkness, or engage in dialogue, demand quality and in doing so lean over and light the candle of hope.

I have in this Oration quoted Regan and Bobby Kennedy. I have drawn from Obama. I have spoken of Fraser and Whitlam, Hawke and Keating. I have drawn on the leadership of Menzies, Curtin and Chifley and of Doc Evatt.

Could we wish to imagine a day 20 years hence when quotes of current leaders where referred to, not in lamentation, but in reference to visions leading us forward, filling us with hope, inspiring us to dream, telling us of things to be done, not because they are easy, but because they hard and require the leading by the power of example?

So back to Rufus' question.

How would I answer his question today, and more importantly, tomorrow? What is the content of our national character going to be?

Rufus: I still have inherent faith that at the end of the day, we the Australian people we <u>can</u> get it right.

I believe that we want again to be inspired, to dream, to debate great ideas. Now is the time for us to demand of those in power that they inspire us.

And let's start our discussions from the point of strength that we now have. Our growth was 1.2% last quarter. Greece:-7%. Our unemployment is 5.2%. US over 9.

We are in the ideal future time zone.

This should be our Golden Time. Despite current equity market turmoil, this should be the time where we debate a bright future. Our choices should be ones of inspiration.

If we are not careful, instead of this being our golden time, it will be our lost opportunity. Instead of being a time where we say 'no', it should be a time where we say 'yes'.

My core message is this: nature abhors a vacuum, and the time limit for the vacuum in quality debate has expired. Our country is not a negative one. We are known as the lucky country. We are not a whinging country; we are one that just gets on with it. Negativity is not part of our national character.

It is us who decides.

We decide who leads us and the circumstances in which they lead.

We can and must 'Make Australia Positive Again'.

Is the Fairy Flag the Landravager?

Introduction

I first wrote this article for publication in Norway in 2005. I hoped that an old Scottish tradition may just solve a Norwegian mystery....

The year 2005 marks the centenary of the restoration of the Norwegian throne, and during this year of celebration, many stories will be retold and many links renewed. But there are some mysteries and links that yet need to be discovered!

Let me take you on a small tour of mystery, in which Bergen sits in the centre. This mystery forever links one Scottish Clan with the Norwegian Crown and Scottish fairies to the Norwegian King.

Nearly one thousand years ago, in 1066, Bergen was both a sprinkling of huts and the chosen place for King Harald Hadrada to launch a war fleet. One can imagine the day when King Harald Hadrada stood above the fjords with his two sons, Olaf and Tostig, and looked down upon the biggest war fleet yet assembled. Two hundred boats and more than 6000 men were under his command.

Safely aboard his boat, packed with his weapons and cloaks, was the King's most prized possession – the Landravager. The Landravager was a white silken flag he had captured back in the days when, as Prince, his father had sent Harald to Constantinople for training. Then, as part of the Emperor's bodyguard force, Harald found himself in Syria, where he captured this flag, and developed the superstitious belief that if unfurled when facing crisis, Harald would be saved from doom.

Harald and his sons left Bergen and sailed for York to meet King Harold of England in battle, and win for Norway influence over that land. As the battle turned against the Norwegian King he called for the unfurling of the Landravager, but the call came too late. A single arrow arched through the sky and pierced the King's eye before his flag could be waved and the battle saved.

We know part of what followed. Harald died. Harold of England won but was so weakened that defeat two weeks later in Hastings, was certain. Tostig returned to found Bergen and take the Norwegian crown. Olaf, the elder son, fled to the Isle of Mann, eventually conquering and ruling that land.

But what of the Landravager? Where did this piece of history go?

If we move forward in time, and visit modern day Dunvegan on the Isle of Skye, Scotland, there is another legend. The Chief of one of the most famous Scottish Clans, the MacLeod's, still lives in the millennium old castle, making it the second oldest continually inhabited castle in Europe.

Above the main fireplace, framed and well protected, is the Fairy Flag.

Ask any MacLeod the flag's history and you will be told of a nurse who left the infant third chief cold in the bottom of the garden. According to legend the fairies wrapped him in a light and magical blanket to keep him warm, and told him that this blanket would save the Clan three times.

"If you face certain defeat, on three occasions you may wave this blanket like a flag, and you will be saved. But be careful, for the fourth time, you will be destroyed", the fairies were to have told him.

Twice in MacLeod history this blanket has been waved as a flag on the battle field, and on both occasions the Clan was saved from certain defeat.

But what of the connection with Norway?

After the battle of Stamford Bridge in York, Olaf, eldest son of Harald, fled then conquered the Isle of Mann. For 200 years his descendants ruled there, until the time of Olaf the Black and the Treaty of Perth. The treaty of Perth provided that Norway lease most of its Scottish lands, including the Isle of Skye, to the government of Britain (and the British paid the rent, right up until the early 1900s).

Reading the writing on the wall, Olaf the Black fostered his son, Leod, to the Sheriff of Skye, to give his son a future in Scotland. After marrying the Sheriff's daughter, Leod became owner of the castle and controller of the lands.

Leod's first two sons, Tormod and Torquil, took on the Scottish form of name where 'Mac' means 'son of'. Tormod and

Torquil adopted the surname 'MacLeod' and a Scottish Clan and tradition were born.

So here is the mystery: Harald Hadrada had his Landravager: A silken flag won in Syria that he believed would save him from defeat in battle. It was not waved in 1066, and vanished, forever.

Yet his eldest son fled to Mann, and his descendants became the MacLeod Clan chiefs, who themselves have a flag they believed was given to them by the fairies 300 years later. This flag would save *them* in battle, but only thrice.

So the direct descendants of King Harald have a flag that sounds like the Landravager, but has attached to it its own Scottish legends. And the Scottish line is genuine and known. This is why, in 1905, the then Chief of MacLeod was asked by the Norwegians to be king, should the Prince Regent refuse.

The Prince Regent did not refuse and we will never now know if the Fairy Flag would have come to Norway, and will never know if such a coming would be a 'homecoming'. But we do know, thanks to modern tests, that the fairy flag is made of 1000 year old Syrian silk!